50 Korean Dish Recipes for Home

By: Kelly Johnson

Table of Contents

- Kimchi
- Bulgogi
- Bibimbap
- Japchae
- Tteokbokki
- Samgyeopsal
- Galbi
- Mandu
- Kimbap
- Sundubu-jjigae
- Jajangmyeon
- Dakgalbi
- Pajeon
- Doenjang-jjigae
- Bossam
- Yukgaejang
- Gimbap
- Naengmyeon
- Haemul Pajeon
- Kimchi jjigae
- Sannakji
- Budae Jjigae
- Dakjuk
- Hobakjuk
- Kongnamul Guk
- Gamjatang
- Dotorimuk
- Gyeranjjim
- Miyeokguk
- Ojingeo bokkeum
- Kimchi fried rice
- Bulgogi bibimbap
- Kimchi pancakes
- Gamja jeon
- Dubu kimchi

- Nakji bokkeum
- Gopchang jeongol
- Haejangguk
- Japchae bap
- Seolleongtang
- Gyeran-mari
- Godeungeo gui
- Dakkochi
- Hobak namul
- Oi muchim
- Oi-naengguk
- Baek kimchi
- Jangjorim
- Kimchi jigae
- Kimchi bokkeumbap

Kimchi

Ingredients:

- 1 large napa cabbage (about 2 pounds)
- 1/2 cup sea salt or kosher salt
- 1 tablespoon grated garlic (about 5-6 cloves)
- 1 teaspoon grated ginger
- 1 teaspoon sugar
- 3-4 tablespoons Korean red chili pepper flakes (gochugaru)
- 4 green onions, chopped
- 1/2 small Korean radish (daikon), peeled and cut into matchsticks
- Optional: 1/4 cup fish sauce or Korean salted shrimp (saeujeot) for added depth of flavor

Instructions:

1. Prepare the Cabbage:
   - Cut the napa cabbage lengthwise into quarters, then chop each quarter into bite-sized pieces.
   - Place the chopped cabbage in a large bowl and sprinkle salt between the leaves, making sure to coat each leaf evenly. Let it sit for 1-2 hours, flipping the cabbage every 30 minutes to ensure even salting. Rinse the cabbage thoroughly under cold water to remove excess salt, then drain well.
2. Make the Kimchi Paste:
   - In a separate bowl, mix the grated garlic, grated ginger, sugar, Korean red chili pepper flakes, and fish sauce or salted shrimp (if using) to form a paste. Adjust the amount of chili flakes based on your desired level of spiciness.
3. Combine Ingredients:
   - Add the chopped green onions and Korean radish matchsticks to the kimchi paste. Mix well until all the vegetables are evenly coated with the paste.
4. Fermentation:
   - Gently massage the kimchi paste into the drained cabbage, making sure each piece is well coated. Pack the kimchi into a clean, airtight jar, pressing down firmly to remove any air bubbles. Leave some space at the top as the kimchi will expand during fermentation.

- Seal the jar tightly and let it ferment at room temperature for 1-2 days. After that, transfer the jar to the refrigerator to slow down the fermentation process. Kimchi will continue to ferment and develop flavor over time.

5. Serve:
    - Enjoy your homemade kimchi as a side dish with rice, or use it to add flavor to various dishes like soups, stews, stir-fries, and kimchi fried rice. Kimchi can be stored in the refrigerator for several weeks to months, depending on your preferred level of fermentation.

Feel free to adjust the ingredients and seasonings according to your taste preferences!

Bulgogi

Ingredients:

- 1 pound of beef (usually sirloin or ribeye), thinly sliced
- 1/2 cup soy sauce
- 1/4 cup brown sugar
- 2 tablespoons sesame oil
- 3 cloves garlic, minced
- 1 teaspoon grated ginger
- 2 tablespoons rice wine (mirin) or dry white wine
- 1 tablespoon sesame seeds (optional)
- 2 green onions, thinly sliced
- 1 medium onion, thinly sliced
- 1 carrot, julienned (optional)
- Cooking oil for grilling or stir-frying

Instructions:

1. Prepare the Marinade:
    - In a bowl, mix together the soy sauce, brown sugar, sesame oil, minced garlic, grated ginger, rice wine, and sesame seeds (if using). Stir until the sugar is dissolved.
2. Marinate the Beef:
    - Place the thinly sliced beef in a shallow dish or a resealable plastic bag. Pour the marinade over the beef, making sure it's evenly coated. Cover the dish or seal the bag and refrigerate for at least 1 hour, or preferably overnight, to allow the flavors to penetrate the meat.
3. Cooking Options:
    - Grilling: Preheat your grill to medium-high heat. Grill the marinated beef slices for 2-3 minutes on each side, or until they are cooked to your desired level of doneness.
    - Stir-frying: Heat a tablespoon of cooking oil in a large skillet or wok over medium-high heat. Add the marinated beef slices along with the sliced onions and carrots (if using). Stir-fry for 3-5 minutes, or until the beef is cooked through and the vegetables are tender.
4. Serve:
    - Garnish the cooked bulgogi with thinly sliced green onions and sesame seeds, if desired. Serve hot with steamed rice and your favorite Korean side dishes, such as kimchi and pickled vegetables.

Bulgogi is a versatile dish that can be enjoyed on its own or used as a filling for lettuce wraps, bibimbap, or Korean-style tacos. Adjust the seasoning and marinating time according to your taste preferences for the perfect balance of sweet, savory, and umami flavors.

Bibimbap

Ingredients:

- 2 cups cooked short-grain white rice
- 1 cup assorted vegetables (such as carrots, spinach, mushrooms, bean sprouts, zucchini), thinly sliced or julienned
- 1/2 pound beef (such as sirloin or ribeye), thinly sliced
- 2 cloves garlic, minced
- 2 tablespoons soy sauce
- 1 tablespoon sesame oil
- 1 tablespoon sugar
- 4 eggs
- 4 tablespoons gochujang (Korean red chili paste)
- Cooking oil
- Salt and pepper to taste
- Toasted sesame seeds for garnish
- Optional: sliced green onions for garnish

Instructions:

1. Prepare the Rice:
    - Cook the short-grain white rice according to package instructions. Once cooked, fluff the rice with a fork and set aside.
2. Prepare the Vegetables:
    - Blanch or sauté the assorted vegetables individually until tender-crisp. Season each vegetable lightly with salt and pepper as they cook. Set aside.
3. Marinate the Beef:
    - In a bowl, combine the thinly sliced beef with minced garlic, soy sauce, sesame oil, and sugar. Mix well and let it marinate for at least 15-20 minutes.
4. Cook the Beef:
    - Heat a skillet or wok over medium-high heat. Add a tablespoon of cooking oil and stir-fry the marinated beef until cooked through, about 3-4 minutes. Remove from heat and set aside.
5. Fry the Eggs:
    - In the same skillet, heat a little more oil over medium heat. Crack the eggs into the skillet and fry them until the whites are set but the yolks are still runny, or to your desired doneness. Remove from heat and set aside.

6. Assemble the Bibimbap:
   - Divide the cooked rice among serving bowls. Arrange the assorted cooked vegetables and cooked beef on top of the rice, placing each ingredient in its own section on the bowl.
   - Place a fried egg on top of each bowl of bibimbap, positioning it in the center.
   - Serve with a dollop of gochujang (Korean red chili paste) on the side.
7. Serve:
   - Sprinkle the bibimbap with toasted sesame seeds and sliced green onions for garnish, if desired.
   - To eat, mix all the ingredients together thoroughly, incorporating the gochujang and egg into the rice and vegetables.

Bibimbap is a customizable dish, so feel free to add or substitute any vegetables or protein according to your preferences. Enjoy the combination of flavors and textures in each bite!

Japchae

Ingredients:

- 200g sweet potato starch noodles (dangmyeon)
- 150g beef (such as sirloin or ribeye), thinly sliced
- 1 onion, thinly sliced
- 1 carrot, julienned
- 1 red bell pepper, julienned
- 1 bunch spinach, washed and trimmed
- 4-5 shiitake mushrooms, thinly sliced
- 4 cloves garlic, minced
- 2 tablespoons soy sauce
- 2 tablespoons sesame oil
- 1 tablespoon sugar
- Toasted sesame seeds for garnish
- Cooking oil
- Salt and pepper to taste

Instructions:

1. Prepare the Sweet Potato Starch Noodles:
    - Cook the sweet potato starch noodles according to the package instructions. Usually, they need to be soaked in warm water for about 10-15 minutes until they become soft, then boiled for 5-7 minutes until they are fully cooked but still chewy. Drain and rinse the noodles under cold water to stop the cooking process. Set aside.
2. Marinate the Beef:
    - In a bowl, combine the thinly sliced beef with minced garlic, soy sauce, sesame oil, and sugar. Mix well and let it marinate for about 15-20 minutes.
3. Prepare the Vegetables:
    - Blanch the spinach in boiling water for about 30 seconds, then immediately transfer it to a bowl of cold water to stop the cooking process. Squeeze out excess water and season lightly with salt and sesame oil.
    - Heat a little cooking oil in a pan over medium heat. Stir-fry the sliced onions, carrots, bell peppers, and shiitake mushrooms until they are tender-crisp. Season with a pinch of salt and pepper. Remove from heat and set aside.

4. Cook the Beef:
   - In the same pan, add a little more oil if needed. Stir-fry the marinated beef until cooked through, about 3-4 minutes. Remove from heat and set aside.
5. Combine Ingredients:
   - In a large mixing bowl, combine the cooked noodles, stir-fried vegetables, and cooked beef. Toss everything together until well combined.
6. Season:
   - Drizzle the japchae with additional sesame oil and sprinkle with toasted sesame seeds. Toss again to evenly distribute the seasoning.
7. Serve:
   - Transfer the japchae to a serving platter or individual plates. Garnish with more sesame seeds if desired.
   - Japchae can be served warm or at room temperature as a side dish or main course. Enjoy the sweet and savory flavors of this delicious Korean noodle dish!

Feel free to adjust the ingredients and seasonings according to your taste preferences. Japchae is a versatile dish, and you can add other vegetables like mushrooms, onions, or even sliced tofu for more variation.

Tteokbokki

Ingredients:

- 200g of cylinder-shaped rice cakes (tteok)
- 2 cups water
- 2 tablespoons gochujang (Korean red chili paste)
- 1 tablespoon soy sauce
- 1 tablespoon sugar
- 1 tablespoon gochugaru (Korean red chili pepper flakes), adjust to taste
- 1 tablespoon sesame oil
- 1 clove garlic, minced
- 1/2 onion, thinly sliced
- 1/2 carrot, thinly sliced
- Optional: 1 hard-boiled egg, sliced
- Optional garnish: chopped green onions, toasted sesame seeds

Instructions:

1. Prepare the Rice Cakes:
    - If your rice cakes are hard, soak them in cold water for about 30 minutes to soften. Drain before using.
2. Make the Sauce:
    - In a small bowl, mix together water, gochujang, soy sauce, sugar, gochugaru, sesame oil, and minced garlic until well combined. Adjust the seasoning to your taste preference, adding more gochugaru for extra spiciness if desired.
3. Cook the Vegetables:
    - Heat a little oil in a large pan or wok over medium heat. Add the sliced onions and carrots and stir-fry for a few minutes until they start to soften.
4. Simmer the Tteok:
    - Pour the prepared sauce into the pan with the vegetables and bring it to a simmer.
    - Add the soaked rice cakes to the simmering sauce. Stir gently to coat the rice cakes evenly with the sauce.
5. Cook Until Tender:
    - Continue to simmer the tteok in the sauce, stirring occasionally, until the rice cakes are tender and have absorbed some of the sauce. This usually takes about 8-10 minutes. If the sauce thickens too much or the rice cakes are still too firm, you can add a little more water as needed.

6. Add Optional Ingredients:
     - If using, add the sliced hard-boiled egg to the pan and let it warm through in the sauce.
7. Serve:
     - Transfer the cooked tteokbokki to a serving dish. Garnish with chopped green onions and toasted sesame seeds for extra flavor and visual appeal.
     - Serve hot as a snack or side dish, and enjoy the deliciously spicy and chewy rice cakes!

Tteokbokki is a versatile dish, and you can customize it by adding other ingredients like fish cakes, cabbage, or ramen noodles. Adjust the level of spiciness according to your preference by adding more or less gochugaru and gochujang.

Samgyeopsal

Ingredients:

- 500g pork belly, thinly sliced
- Salt
- Black pepper
- Lettuce leaves
- Perilla leaves (optional)
- Ssamjang (Korean dipping sauce)
- Kimchi
- Garlic cloves, peeled
- Sesame oil
- Optional: sliced green onions, sliced chili peppers

Instructions:

1. Prepare the Pork Belly:
    - If the pork belly slices are too large, you can cut them into smaller pieces for easier cooking.
    - Season both sides of the pork belly slices with a pinch of salt and black pepper.
2. Prepare the Accompaniments:
    - Rinse the lettuce leaves and perilla leaves (if using) and pat them dry. Arrange them on a serving plate along with the ssamjang (Korean dipping sauce), kimchi, and peeled garlic cloves.
    - You can also prepare additional garnishes like sliced green onions and chili peppers if desired.
3. Grill the Pork Belly:
    - Heat a grill pan or barbecue grill over medium-high heat. Once hot, place the seasoned pork belly slices on the grill.
    - Grill the pork belly for 2-3 minutes on each side, or until cooked through and nicely charred. Adjust the cooking time as needed depending on the thickness of the slices.
    - Be careful not to overcook the pork belly to prevent it from becoming tough and dry.
4. Serve:
    - Transfer the grilled pork belly slices to a serving plate.

- To eat, take a piece of lettuce or perilla leaf and place a grilled pork belly slice on top. Add a small dollop of ssamjang, a piece of garlic, and any other desired garnishes such as kimchi, green onions, or chili peppers.
- Wrap the ingredients in the lettuce or perilla leaf and enjoy it as a delicious and flavorful bite-sized wrap.

5. Enjoy:
    - Enjoy the samgyeopsal wraps with a side of kimchi and any other Korean side dishes you like.
    - You can also drizzle some sesame oil over the grilled pork belly slices for extra flavor before wrapping them in the lettuce or perilla leaves.

Samgyeopsal is a fun and interactive dish to enjoy with family and friends, perfect for gatherings and celebrations. Adjust the seasonings and accompaniments according to your taste preferences for a personalized dining experience.

Galbi

Ingredients:

- 2 pounds beef short ribs (flanken-cut or English-cut)
- 1/2 cup soy sauce
- 1/4 cup brown sugar
- 2 tablespoons sesame oil
- 4 cloves garlic, minced
- 1 tablespoon grated ginger
- 2 green onions, chopped
- 1 small pear, grated (optional, for sweetness)
- 1 tablespoon sesame seeds
- 1/4 teaspoon black pepper
- Optional: sliced onion, carrot, and mushrooms for grilling

Instructions:

1. Prepare the Marinade:
    - In a bowl, combine soy sauce, brown sugar, sesame oil, minced garlic, grated ginger, chopped green onions, grated pear (if using), sesame seeds, and black pepper. Mix well until the sugar is dissolved and the ingredients are thoroughly combined.
2. Marinate the Ribs:
    - Place the beef short ribs in a shallow dish or resealable plastic bag. Pour the marinade over the ribs, making sure they are evenly coated. Marinate the ribs in the refrigerator for at least 4 hours, or preferably overnight, to allow the flavors to penetrate the meat.
3. Prepare the Grill:
    - Preheat your grill to medium-high heat. If using a charcoal grill, wait until the coals are hot and glowing.
4. Grill the Ribs:
    - Remove the marinated ribs from the refrigerator and let them sit at room temperature for about 20-30 minutes before grilling.
    - Place the ribs on the preheated grill, making sure to shake off any excess marinade. Grill the ribs for 3-4 minutes on each side, or until they are cooked to your desired level of doneness and have nice grill marks.
    - If desired, grill sliced onion, carrot, and mushrooms alongside the ribs for additional flavor and variety.
5. Serve:

- Transfer the grilled galbi to a serving platter and garnish with additional chopped green onions and sesame seeds if desired.
- Serve hot with steamed rice and your favorite Korean side dishes, such as kimchi, pickled vegetables, and lettuce leaves for wrapping.
- Enjoy the succulent and flavorful Korean BBQ short ribs with family and friends!

Galbi is a versatile dish that can also be cooked indoors using a grill pan or broiler. Adjust the cooking time and temperature accordingly if using different cuts of meat or cooking methods.

Mandu

Ingredients:

For the Filling:

- 1 pound ground pork or beef
- 1 cup finely chopped cabbage
- 1/2 cup chopped green onions
- 1/4 cup chopped onion
- 2 cloves garlic, minced
- 1 tablespoon soy sauce
- 1 tablespoon sesame oil
- 1 teaspoon sugar
- 1/2 teaspoon black pepper
- Optional: 1/4 cup chopped tofu (firm or extra firm), drained
- Optional: 1/4 cup chopped mushrooms (such as shiitake or button mushrooms), sautéed

For the Dumpling Wrappers:

- 1 package round dumpling wrappers (also known as mandu or gyoza wrappers)
- Water (for sealing the wrappers)

For Cooking:

- Cooking oil (for pan-frying) or water (for boiling or steaming)
- Optional: Dipping sauce (such as soy sauce mixed with rice vinegar, sesame oil, and a touch of sugar)

Instructions:

1. Prepare the Filling:
    - In a large mixing bowl, combine the ground meat, chopped cabbage, green onions, onion, minced garlic, soy sauce, sesame oil, sugar, black pepper, and any optional ingredients like chopped tofu or mushrooms. Mix until all the ingredients are well combined.
2. Assemble the Dumplings:

- Take a dumpling wrapper and place a small spoonful of the filling in the center. Dip your finger in water and moisten the edges of the wrapper.
- Fold the wrapper in half to form a half-moon shape, then pinch the edges together to seal the dumpling. You can crimp the edges to create a decorative pattern if desired. Repeat with the remaining wrappers and filling.

3. Cook the Dumplings:
   - Pan-Frying: Heat a tablespoon of cooking oil in a large non-stick skillet over medium heat. Place the dumplings in the skillet, making sure they're not touching each other. Cook for 2-3 minutes, or until the bottoms are golden brown. Add about 1/4 cup of water to the skillet, cover with a lid, and steam the dumplings for an additional 5-6 minutes, or until the filling is cooked through and the wrappers are translucent.
   - Boiling: Bring a large pot of water to a boil. Carefully add the dumplings to the boiling water and cook for 5-6 minutes, or until they float to the surface and the filling is cooked through.
   - Steaming: Arrange the dumplings in a single layer in a steamer basket lined with parchment paper or cabbage leaves. Steam the dumplings for 10-12 minutes, or until the filling is cooked through and the wrappers are soft and tender.

4. Serve:
   - Serve the cooked mandu hot with dipping sauce on the side. Enjoy the delicious Korean dumplings as a snack, appetizer, or part of a larger meal.

Feel free to customize the filling according to your preferences by adding or substituting ingredients like shrimp, tofu, mushrooms, or additional vegetables. Mandu can also be frozen before cooking for later use; simply arrange the assembled dumplings in a single layer on a baking sheet and freeze until firm, then transfer them to a freezer bag or container for storage.

Kimbap

Ingredients:

For the Rice:

- 2 cups sushi rice (short-grain white rice)
- 2 1/2 cups water
- 3 tablespoons rice vinegar
- 1 tablespoon sugar
- 1 teaspoon salt

For the Fillings:

- 5-6 sheets of roasted seaweed (nori)
- 3-4 strips of cooked ham or spam, cut into thin strips
- 2 eggs, beaten and scrambled
- 1 carrot, julienned and sautéed
- 1/2 cucumber, julienned
- 5-6 imitation crab sticks
- 1 bunch spinach, blanched and squeezed dry
- Sesame oil (for brushing)

Optional Fillings:

- Pickled radish (danmuji)
- Stir-fried fish cake (eomuk)
- Kimchi
- Avocado slices
- Tuna salad

Instructions:

1. Prepare the Rice:
    - Rinse the sushi rice under cold water until the water runs clear. Combine the rice and water in a rice cooker and cook according to the manufacturer's instructions.
    - In a small saucepan, heat the rice vinegar, sugar, and salt over low heat until the sugar and salt are dissolved. Once the rice is cooked, transfer it to

a large mixing bowl and gently fold in the vinegar mixture until well combined. Let the rice cool slightly.
2. Prepare the Fillings:
    - Cook the eggs in a non-stick skillet over medium heat, stirring occasionally, until scrambled. Set aside.
    - Julienne the carrots and cucumber, then sauté the carrots in a little oil until tender-crisp. Blanch the spinach in boiling water for 30 seconds, then drain and squeeze out excess water.
    - Cut the imitation crab sticks into thin strips.
3. Assemble the Kimbap:
    - Place a bamboo sushi mat on a clean work surface and cover it with plastic wrap. Lay a sheet of roasted seaweed (nori) on top of the plastic wrap, shiny side down.
    - Spread a thin layer of seasoned rice evenly over the seaweed, leaving a 1-inch border along the top edge.
    - Arrange the fillings in a single layer across the center of the rice, leaving some space at the top. Be careful not to overfill.
    - Starting from the bottom edge, tightly roll the kimbap using the bamboo mat, pressing gently to shape it as you roll. Seal the edge by moistening it with a little water.
    - Brush the outside of the kimbap lightly with sesame oil for added flavor and to prevent the seaweed from becoming too dry.
4. Slice and Serve:
    - Use a sharp knife to slice the rolled kimbap into bite-sized pieces, about 1-inch thick.
    - Serve the sliced kimbap with dipping sauce such as soy sauce mixed with a little rice vinegar and sesame oil, if desired.

Kimbap is a versatile dish, so feel free to customize the fillings according to your preferences. You can also wrap the kimbap in plastic wrap and store it in the refrigerator for later use or pack it for a picnic or lunchbox. Enjoy the delicious Korean flavors of homemade kimbap!

Sundubu-jjigae

Ingredients:

- 1 package (about 14 oz) soft tofu (sundubu)
- 1/2 onion, sliced
- 2 cloves garlic, minced
- 1 green onion, chopped
- 1/2 cup sliced mushrooms (such as shiitake or button mushrooms)
- 1/2 cup sliced zucchini
- 1/4 cup sliced carrot
- 1/4 cup chopped kimchi (optional, for extra flavor)
- 1/2 cup seafood (such as shrimp, clams, or mussels) or thinly sliced beef or pork (optional)
- 2 cups anchovy or vegetable broth
- 2 tablespoons gochujang (Korean red chili paste)
- 1 tablespoon soy sauce
- 1 tablespoon sesame oil
- 1 tablespoon cooking oil
- Salt and pepper to taste
- 1 egg (optional)
- 1 tablespoon chopped green onion (for garnish)
- Toasted sesame seeds (for garnish)

Instructions:

1. Prepare the Ingredients:
    - Drain the soft tofu and cut it into bite-sized cubes. Set aside.
    - Heat a tablespoon of cooking oil in a large pot or deep skillet over medium heat. Add the minced garlic and sliced onion, and sauté until fragrant, about 1-2 minutes.
2. Add the Vegetables:
    - Add the sliced mushrooms, zucchini, carrot, and chopped kimchi (if using) to the pot. Stir-fry for another 2-3 minutes until the vegetables are slightly softened.
3. Add the Broth and Seasonings:
    - Pour the anchovy or vegetable broth into the pot and bring it to a simmer. Add the gochujang (Korean red chili paste), soy sauce, and sesame oil. Stir well to combine.
4. Add the Tofu and Protein (if using):

- Carefully add the cubed soft tofu to the simmering broth. If using seafood, beef, or pork, add it to the pot at this time as well. Gently stir to incorporate the ingredients.

5. Simmer the Stew:
   - Let the sundubu-jjigae simmer gently for about 5-7 minutes, or until the tofu is heated through and the seafood or meat is cooked. Season with salt and pepper to taste.
6. Optional: Add an Egg:
   - If desired, crack an egg into the center of the stew. Allow the egg to cook in the hot broth until the whites are set but the yolk is still runny.
7. Serve:
   - Garnish the sundubu-jjigae with chopped green onion and toasted sesame seeds.
   - Serve hot with steamed rice and additional side dishes if desired.

Sundubu-jjigae is a comforting and satisfying dish, perfect for warming up on cold days or enjoying any time you're craving a spicy and flavorful Korean stew. Feel free to adjust the level of spiciness by adding more or less gochujang according to your taste preferences. Enjoy!

Jajangmyeon

Ingredients:

For the Black Bean Sauce (Jajang):

- 200g pork belly or pork shoulder, diced
- 1 tablespoon vegetable oil
- 1 tablespoon sesame oil
- 1 onion, finely chopped
- 2 cloves garlic, minced
- 1 tablespoon grated ginger
- 1/2 cup black bean paste (chunjang)
- 1 tablespoon sugar
- 1 tablespoon soy sauce
- 2 cups water
- 2 tablespoons cornstarch mixed with 2 tablespoons water (optional, for thickening)

For the Noodles:

- 400g fresh or dried noodles (such as wheat noodles or udon noodles)
- 1 tablespoon vegetable oil (for cooking the noodles)
- Optional: cucumber or radish slices, for garnish

Instructions:

1. Prepare the Black Bean Sauce (Jajang):
    - Heat vegetable oil and sesame oil in a large skillet or wok over medium heat. Add the diced pork and cook until browned and cooked through.
    - Add chopped onion, minced garlic, and grated ginger to the skillet. Stir-fry until the onion is softened and aromatic.
    - Add black bean paste (chunjang) to the skillet and stir-fry with the pork and vegetables for a couple of minutes.
    - Stir in sugar and soy sauce, then gradually pour in 2 cups of water, stirring constantly to combine. Bring the mixture to a simmer and let it cook for 5-7 minutes, allowing the flavors to meld.

- If you prefer a thicker sauce, stir in the cornstarch mixture and cook for an additional 1-2 minutes until the sauce thickens. Remove from heat and set aside.
2. Cook the Noodles:
   - Bring a large pot of water to a boil. Add the fresh or dried noodles and cook according to the package instructions until al dente. Drain the noodles and rinse them under cold water to stop the cooking process. Drain well.
   - Heat a tablespoon of vegetable oil in a large skillet or wok over medium heat. Add the cooked noodles to the skillet and stir-fry for 1-2 minutes until heated through and evenly coated with oil.
3. Assemble the Jajangmyeon:
   - Divide the cooked noodles among serving bowls. Ladle the prepared black bean sauce (jajang) over the noodles, covering them evenly.
   - Garnish with cucumber or radish slices if desired.
4. Serve:
   - Serve the jajangmyeon hot and enjoy!

Jajangmyeon is typically served with a side of pickled radish and kimchi. It's a hearty and flavorful dish that's perfect for satisfying your cravings for comforting noodles. Adjust the seasoning and thickness of the sauce according to your taste preferences. Enjoy!

Dakgalbi

Ingredients:

For the Marinade:

- 500g boneless, skinless chicken thighs, cut into bite-sized pieces
- 3 tablespoons gochujang (Korean red chili paste)
- 2 tablespoons soy sauce
- 1 tablespoon honey or sugar
- 1 tablespoon sesame oil
- 1 tablespoon grated ginger
- 2 cloves garlic, minced
- 1 teaspoon black pepper

For the Stir-Fry:

- 2 tablespoons vegetable oil
- 1 onion, thinly sliced
- 1 sweet potato, thinly sliced
- 1 carrot, thinly sliced
- 2 cups cabbage, thinly sliced
- 2-3 green onions, cut into 2-inch pieces
- Optional: 1 cup sliced mushrooms (such as shiitake or button mushrooms)

For Garnish (Optional):

- Sesame seeds
- Chopped green onions

For Serving (Optional):

- Cooked rice
- Lettuce leaves for wrapping

Instructions:

1. Marinate the Chicken:

- In a bowl, combine the chicken pieces with gochujang, soy sauce, honey or sugar, sesame oil, grated ginger, minced garlic, and black pepper. Mix well until the chicken is evenly coated. Cover and refrigerate for at least 30 minutes to allow the flavors to meld.
2. Prepare the Vegetables:
    - Heat a large skillet or wok over medium heat. Add the vegetable oil.
    - Add the sliced onion, sweet potato, carrot, and cabbage to the skillet. Stir-fry for a few minutes until the vegetables start to soften.
3. Stir-Fry the Chicken:
    - Push the vegetables to the side of the skillet to create a space in the center. Add the marinated chicken to the center of the skillet. Cook, stirring occasionally, until the chicken is cooked through and no longer pink, about 6-8 minutes.
4. Combine Everything:
    - Once the chicken is cooked, mix it with the vegetables in the skillet. Add the green onions and sliced mushrooms (if using). Stir-fry for an additional 2-3 minutes, until everything is heated through and well combined.
5. Garnish and Serve:
    - Garnish the dakgalbi with sesame seeds and chopped green onions, if desired.
    - Serve hot with cooked rice on the side or wrap the dakgalbi in lettuce leaves for a lighter option.

Dakgalbi is a versatile dish, so feel free to customize it by adding or substituting vegetables and adjusting the level of spiciness according to your taste preferences.

Enjoy the delicious flavors of homemade dakgalbi!

Pajeon

Ingredients:

- 2 cups all-purpose flour
- 2 cups water
- 1 egg
- 2 cups chopped scallions (green onions), both green and white parts
- 1/2 cup chopped kimchi (optional, for extra flavor)
- 1/2 cup small shrimp or chopped cooked pork (optional, for protein)
- 1 tablespoon soy sauce
- 1 tablespoon sesame oil
- Vegetable oil, for frying
- Soy dipping sauce (for serving)

Instructions:

1. **Prepare the Batter:**
   - In a large mixing bowl, whisk together the all-purpose flour, water, and egg until smooth and well combined. The consistency should be similar to pancake batter. If it's too thick, you can add a little more water.
2. **Add the Scallions and Optional Ingredients:**
   - Stir in the chopped scallions, kimchi (if using), small shrimp or chopped cooked pork (if using), soy sauce, and sesame oil. Mix until the ingredients are evenly distributed throughout the batter.
3. **Heat the Pan:**
   - Heat a non-stick skillet or frying pan over medium heat. Add a tablespoon of vegetable oil and swirl to coat the bottom of the pan evenly.
4. **Cook the Pancake:**
   - Pour a ladleful of the batter into the heated skillet, spreading it out evenly into a round shape with the back of the ladle.
   - Cook the pancake for 3-4 minutes on one side, or until the bottom is golden brown and crispy.
5. **Flip and Cook the Other Side:**
   - Carefully flip the pancake using a spatula. Add a little more oil around the edges if needed.
   - Cook for an additional 3-4 minutes on the other side, until golden brown and crispy.
6. **Repeat:**

        - Repeat the process with the remaining batter, adding more oil to the skillet as needed between batches.
7. Serve:
        - Once cooked, transfer the pajeon to a serving plate. Cut into wedges and serve hot with soy dipping sauce on the side.

Pajeon is best enjoyed hot and crispy, straight from the pan. It's delicious on its own or paired with a variety of side dishes. Feel free to customize the recipe by adding other ingredients such as seafood, vegetables, or even cheese. Enjoy your homemade pajeon!

Doenjang-jjigae

Ingredients:

- 1/4 cup fermented soybean paste (doenjang)
- 4 cups water or anchovy stock
- 1/2 onion, thinly sliced
- 1 small zucchini, sliced into rounds
- 1 small potato, peeled and diced
- 1/2 cup sliced mushrooms (such as shiitake or button mushrooms)
- 1/2 cup cubed tofu
- 2 cloves garlic, minced
- 1 green chili pepper, thinly sliced (optional, for heat)
- 2 green onions, chopped
- 1 tablespoon vegetable oil
- Salt and pepper to taste

Instructions:

1. Prepare the Ingredients:
    - In a small bowl, dissolve the fermented soybean paste (doenjang) in a little water to make a smooth paste. Set aside.
    - Prepare the vegetables by slicing the onion, zucchini, and mushrooms, and dicing the potato. Drain and cube the tofu.
2. Saute the Aromatics:
    - Heat vegetable oil in a large pot or deep skillet over medium heat. Add minced garlic and sliced green chili pepper (if using), and sauté for a minute until fragrant.
3. Add the Vegetables:
    - Add the sliced onion, zucchini, potato, and mushrooms to the pot. Stir-fry for a few minutes until the vegetables start to soften.
4. Make the Soup Base:
    - Pour the water or anchovy stock into the pot with the vegetables. Bring it to a simmer.
5. Add the Doenjang Paste:
    - Gradually add the dissolved doenjang paste to the simmering soup, stirring constantly to incorporate it evenly. Let the soup simmer for about 10-15 minutes to allow the flavors to meld and the vegetables to cook through.
6. Add the Tofu and Green Onions:

- Once the vegetables are tender, add the cubed tofu and chopped green onions to the pot. Simmer for an additional 5 minutes.
7. Adjust Seasoning:
    - Taste the stew and adjust the seasoning with salt and pepper as needed. The doenjang paste is already salty, so be cautious with the amount of additional salt you add.
8. Serve:
    - Ladle the hot doenjang-jjigae into individual bowls and serve immediately.
    - Enjoy the hearty and comforting flavors of homemade doenjang-jjigae, perfect for warming up on chilly days!

Doenjang-jjigae can be customized with a variety of vegetables and protein sources according to your preferences. It's often served with a bowl of steamed rice and other Korean side dishes for a complete meal. Feel free to experiment with different ingredients and adjust the seasoning to suit your taste.

Bossam

Ingredients:

For the Pork Belly:

- 1.5-2 pounds pork belly
- 1 onion, peeled and quartered
- 4 cloves garlic, peeled
- 2-3 green onions, cut into large pieces
- 1 tablespoon whole black peppercorns
- 1 tablespoon soy sauce
- Water

For Serving:

- Thinly sliced radish or lettuce leaves
- Ssamjang (Korean dipping sauce)
- Sliced garlic
- Sliced green chili peppers
- Kimchi
- Rice
- Additional side dishes as desired

Instructions:

1. Prepare the Pork Belly:
    - Rinse the pork belly under cold water and pat it dry with paper towels. Place it in a large pot or Dutch oven.
    - Add the quartered onion, garlic cloves, green onions, black peppercorns, and soy sauce to the pot with the pork belly.
    - Pour enough water into the pot to cover the pork belly by about an inch.
2. Boil the Pork Belly:
    - Bring the pot to a boil over high heat. Once boiling, reduce the heat to low and let the pork belly simmer gently, partially covered, for 1.5 to 2 hours, or until the meat is tender and easily pierced with a fork.
3. Remove and Slice the Pork Belly:
    - Carefully remove the pork belly from the pot and transfer it to a cutting board. Let it rest for a few minutes.

- Slice the pork belly into thin pieces, about 1/4-inch thick. You can slice it across the grain for a more tender texture.
4. Serve:
    - Arrange the thinly sliced radish or lettuce leaves on a serving platter.
    - Place the sliced pork belly on top of the radish or lettuce leaves.
    - Serve with ssamjang (Korean dipping sauce), sliced garlic, sliced green chili peppers, kimchi, rice, and any additional side dishes you like.
5. Wrap and Enjoy:
    - To eat, take a piece of radish or lettuce leaf and place a slice of pork belly on top. Add a small spoonful of ssamjang, sliced garlic, sliced green chili peppers, and any other desired condiments or side dishes.
    - Wrap everything together and enjoy the delicious flavors of bossam!

Bossam is a customizable dish, so feel free to adjust the condiments and side dishes according to your taste preferences. It's a satisfying and flavorful meal that's perfect for sharing with family and friends.

Yukgaejang

Ingredients:

For the Beef Broth:

- 500g beef brisket or flank steak, thinly sliced
- 8 cups water
- 1 onion, halved
- 4 cloves garlic, crushed
- 4 green onions, cut into large pieces
- 1 tablespoon soy sauce
- Salt to taste

For the Soup:

- 1 tablespoon vegetable oil
- 1 onion, thinly sliced
- 4 cloves garlic, minced
- 1 tablespoon gochugaru (Korean red chili flakes)
- 2 tablespoons soy sauce
- 1 tablespoon fish sauce
- 1 tablespoon sesame oil
- 6 cups beef broth (from above)
- 2 cups shredded napa cabbage
- 1 cup sliced mushrooms (such as shiitake or button mushrooms)
- 1 cup sliced carrots
- 1 cup soaked and drained fernbrake (gosari)
- 1 cup soaked and drained sliced dried radish greens (mu namul)
- 1 cup sliced green onions
- 1 cup cooked glass noodles (optional)
- Salt and pepper to taste

For Garnish (Optional):

- Thinly sliced green onions
- Toasted sesame seeds

Instructions:

1. Prepare the Beef Broth:
   - In a large pot, combine the beef slices, water, halved onion, crushed garlic cloves, green onions, soy sauce, and a pinch of salt. Bring to a boil over high heat.
   - Once boiling, reduce the heat to low and simmer, partially covered, for about 1.5 to 2 hours, or until the beef is tender and the broth is flavorful.
   - Strain the broth, discarding the solids. Set the broth aside.
2. Prepare the Soup:
   - Heat vegetable oil in a large pot or Dutch oven over medium heat. Add the thinly sliced onion and minced garlic, and sauté until softened and fragrant.
   - Stir in the gochugaru (Korean red chili flakes), soy sauce, fish sauce, and sesame oil. Cook for another minute.
   - Pour in the beef broth, and bring the soup to a boil.
3. Add Vegetables and Beef:
   - Add the shredded napa cabbage, sliced mushrooms, sliced carrots, soaked and drained fernbrake, soaked and drained sliced dried radish greens, and sliced green onions to the pot.
   - Once the soup returns to a boil, reduce the heat to low and simmer for about 20-30 minutes, or until the vegetables are tender and cooked through.
4. Add Noodles (Optional) and Adjust Seasoning:
   - If using cooked glass noodles, add them to the pot and simmer for an additional 5 minutes.
   - Taste the soup and adjust the seasoning with salt and pepper as needed.
5. Serve:
   - Ladle the hot yukgaejang into individual serving bowls.
   - Garnish with thinly sliced green onions and toasted sesame seeds if desired.
   - Serve hot and enjoy the spicy and comforting flavors of homemade yukgaejang!

Yukgaejang is a versatile dish, so feel free to adjust the ingredients and level of spiciness according to your taste preferences. It's often served with a bowl of steamed rice and additional side dishes for a complete meal.

Gimbap

Ingredients:

For the Rice:

- 3 cups cooked short-grain white rice
- 2 tablespoons rice vinegar
- 1 tablespoon sugar
- 1 teaspoon salt

For the Fillings:

- 5-6 sheets of roasted seaweed (nori)
- 1 carrot, julienned and sautéed
- 1/2 cucumber, julienned
- 1/2 cup spinach, blanched and squeezed dry
- 3-4 strips of cooked ham or imitation crab sticks
- 3-4 strips of omelette (made from 2 eggs)
- 1 tablespoon sesame oil
- Salt and pepper to taste

For Assembly:

- Bamboo sushi mat
- Sesame oil (for brushing)
- Sesame seeds (for garnish)
- Soy sauce, wasabi, and pickled radish (for serving)

Instructions:

1. Prepare the Rice:
    - In a small bowl, mix together rice vinegar, sugar, and salt until dissolved.
    - Add the cooked rice to a large mixing bowl and pour the vinegar mixture over it. Gently fold the rice with a spatula to evenly distribute the seasoning. Let the rice cool to room temperature.
2. Prepare the Fillings:
    - Julienne the carrot and cucumber. Sauté the julienned carrot in a bit of oil until tender-crisp.

- Blanch the spinach in boiling water for 30 seconds, then drain and squeeze out excess water.
- Cook the ham or imitation crab sticks if they're not already cooked.
- Make a thin omelette using the eggs seasoned with salt and pepper, then slice into strips.

3. Assemble the Gimbap:
    - Place a sheet of roasted seaweed (nori) on a bamboo sushi mat, shiny side down.
    - Spread a thin layer of seasoned rice evenly over the seaweed, leaving about 1-inch of space at the top edge.
    - Arrange the fillings (carrot, cucumber, spinach, ham or crab sticks, and omelette strips) in a line across the center of the rice.
4. Roll the Gimbap:
    - Starting from the bottom edge closest to you, lift the bamboo mat with your thumbs and roll it away from you, enclosing the fillings in the rice and seaweed.
    - Press gently but firmly on the bamboo mat as you roll to ensure the gimbap is tightly packed.
    - Once rolled, brush the top edge of the seaweed with a little sesame oil to seal the roll.
5. Slice and Garnish:
    - Use a sharp knife to slice the rolled gimbap into bite-sized pieces, about 1-inch thick.
    - Garnish the gimbap with sesame seeds sprinkled over the top.
6. Serve:
    - Serve the sliced gimbap with soy sauce, wasabi, and pickled radish on the side for dipping.

Gimbap is a delicious and customizable dish, so feel free to add or substitute fillings according to your preferences. It's a fun and satisfying meal to make at home, perfect for sharing with family and friends!

Naengmyeon

Ingredients:

For Mul Naengmyeon:

For the Broth:

- 4 cups beef or chicken broth
- 2 tablespoons soy sauce
- 2 tablespoons rice vinegar
- 1 tablespoon sugar
- 1 tablespoon sesame oil
- 2 cloves garlic, minced
- 1 teaspoon grated ginger
- Salt and pepper to taste

For Serving:

- Cooked naengmyeon noodles (buckwheat noodles)
- Thinly sliced beef or boiled egg (optional)
- Cucumber, julienned
- Asian pear, julienned
- Hard-boiled egg, sliced
- Ice cubes (for serving)

For Bibim Naengmyeon:

For the Sauce:

- 2 tablespoons gochujang (Korean red chili paste)
- 1 tablespoon soy sauce
- 1 tablespoon rice vinegar
- 1 tablespoon sugar
- 1 tablespoon sesame oil
- 2 cloves garlic, minced
- 1 teaspoon grated ginger

For Serving:

- Cooked naengmyeon noodles (buckwheat noodles)
- Thinly sliced beef or boiled egg (optional)
- Cucumber, julienned
- Asian pear, julienned
- Hard-boiled egg, sliced
- Sesame seeds (for garnish)

Instructions:

For Mul Naengmyeon:

1. Prepare the Broth:
    - In a mixing bowl, combine beef or chicken broth with soy sauce, rice vinegar, sugar, sesame oil, minced garlic, grated ginger, salt, and pepper. Adjust seasoning to taste.
    - Chill the broth in the refrigerator until cold.
2. Prepare the Toppings:
    - Prepare the toppings by thinly slicing the beef or boiling the egg (if using), and julienning the cucumber and Asian pear.
    - Cook the naengmyeon noodles according to the package instructions, then rinse under cold water until cool. Drain well.
3. Assemble:
    - Divide the chilled broth among serving bowls. Add the cooked naengmyeon noodles.
    - Top with sliced beef or boiled egg, julienned cucumber and Asian pear, and a few ice cubes for extra chilliness.
4. Serve:
    - Serve the mul naengmyeon cold, with additional vinegar or mustard on the side if desired.

For Bibim Naengmyeon:

1. Prepare the Sauce:
    - In a mixing bowl, whisk together gochujang, soy sauce, rice vinegar, sugar, sesame oil, minced garlic, and grated ginger until well combined.
2. Prepare the Toppings and Noodles:
    - Prepare the toppings and noodles as described in the mul naengmyeon instructions.
3. Mix:

        - Toss the cooked naengmyeon noodles with the prepared sauce until evenly coated.
    4. Assemble:
        - Divide the sauced noodles among serving bowls. Top with sliced beef or boiled egg (if using), julienned cucumber and Asian pear.
    5. Garnish:
        - Garnish with sesame seeds for extra flavor and texture.
    6. Serve:
        - Serve the bibim naengmyeon cold, with additional sauce on the side for those who prefer it spicier.

Naengmyeon is a refreshing and satisfying dish, perfect for cooling off during hot weather. Feel free to customize the toppings and adjust the seasoning according to your taste preferences. Enjoy!

Haemul Pajeon

Ingredients:

For the Pancake Batter:

- 1 cup all-purpose flour
- 1 cup water
- 1 egg
- 1 tablespoon soy sauce
- 1 tablespoon sesame oil
- Salt and pepper to taste

For the Filling:

- Assorted seafood (such as shrimp, squid, and/or mussels), cleaned and chopped into bite-sized pieces
- 4-5 green onions, cut into long strips

For Cooking:

- Vegetable oil for frying

For Dipping Sauce:

- 2 tablespoons soy sauce
- 1 tablespoon rice vinegar
- 1 teaspoon sesame oil
- 1 teaspoon sugar
- 1 teaspoon sesame seeds
- 1 clove garlic, minced (optional)
- Thinly sliced green onions (optional)

Instructions:

1. Prepare the Pancake Batter:
    - In a mixing bowl, combine the all-purpose flour, water, egg, soy sauce, sesame oil, salt, and pepper. Whisk until smooth and well combined. The

batter should have a similar consistency to pancake batter. If it's too thick, you can add a little more water.
2. **Prepare the Filling:**
   - Heat a little vegetable oil in a skillet over medium heat. Add the assorted seafood and stir-fry for a few minutes until cooked through. Remove from heat and set aside.
3. **Combine Batter and Filling:**
   - Add the cooked seafood and sliced green onions to the pancake batter. Stir until the seafood and green onions are evenly distributed throughout the batter.
4. **Cook the Pancake:**
   - Heat a large non-stick skillet or frying pan over medium-high heat. Add a generous amount of vegetable oil to coat the bottom of the skillet.
   - Pour a ladleful of the pancake batter into the skillet, spreading it out evenly into a round shape with the back of the ladle.
   - Cook the pancake for 3-4 minutes on one side, or until the bottom is golden brown and crispy.
5. **Flip and Cook the Other Side:**
   - Carefully flip the pancake using a spatula. Add a little more oil around the edges if needed.
   - Cook for an additional 3-4 minutes on the other side, until golden brown and crispy.
6. **Repeat:**
   - Repeat the process with the remaining batter and filling, adding more oil to the skillet as needed between batches.
7. **Make the Dipping Sauce:**
   - In a small bowl, combine soy sauce, rice vinegar, sesame oil, sugar, sesame seeds, and minced garlic (if using). Stir until the sugar is dissolved.
8. **Serve:**
   - Cut the cooked haemul pajeon into wedges and serve hot, with the dipping sauce on the side.

Haemul pajeon is best enjoyed hot and crispy, straight from the pan. It's a delicious and satisfying dish that's perfect for sharing with family and friends. Enjoy!

Kimchi jjigae

Ingredients:

- 2 cups well-fermented kimchi, chopped
- 200g pork belly or pork shoulder, thinly sliced
- 1 onion, sliced
- 2 cloves garlic, minced
- 1 tablespoon gochugaru (Korean red chili pepper flakes)
- 1 tablespoon gochujang (Korean red chili paste)
- 1 tablespoon soy sauce
- 1 tablespoon sesame oil
- 1 tablespoon vegetable oil
- 2 cups kimchi juice (from the jar of kimchi)
- 2 cups water or anchovy stock
- 1 block firm tofu, cut into cubes
- 2 green onions, chopped
- Salt and pepper to taste

Instructions:

1. Prepare the Ingredients:
    - Chop the well-fermented kimchi into bite-sized pieces.
    - Slice the pork belly or pork shoulder thinly.
    - Slice the onion and mince the garlic.
    - Cut the firm tofu into cubes.
    - Chop the green onions.
2. Saute the Aromatics:
    - Heat vegetable oil in a large pot or a deep skillet over medium heat.
    - Add sliced pork belly or pork shoulder to the pot and cook until lightly browned.
3. Add Kimchi and Seasonings:
    - Add chopped kimchi, sliced onion, and minced garlic to the pot. Stir-fry for a few minutes until the kimchi is slightly softened and aromatic.
    - Add gochugaru (Korean red chili pepper flakes), gochujang (Korean red chili paste), soy sauce, and sesame oil. Stir well to combine.
4. Add Liquid:
    - Pour in kimchi juice (from the jar of kimchi) and water or anchovy stock. Bring the mixture to a boil.
5. Simmer:

- Reduce the heat to medium-low and let the stew simmer for about 20-30 minutes, allowing the flavors to meld together.
6. Add Tofu and Green Onions:
    - Add cubed firm tofu to the stew and gently stir to incorporate.
    - Let the stew simmer for an additional 5-10 minutes, or until the tofu is heated through.
    - Add chopped green onions to the stew and stir.
7. Adjust Seasoning:
    - Taste the kimchi jjigae and adjust the seasoning with salt and pepper if needed. The kimchi and kimchi juice can be salty, so be mindful of the salt content.
8. Serve:
    - Serve the kimchi jjigae hot in individual bowls.
    - Optionally, garnish with additional chopped green onions.
    - Enjoy your comforting and flavorful bowl of kimchi jjigae!

Kimchi jjigae is often served with a bowl of steamed rice and other Korean side dishes for a complete meal. Feel free to adjust the spiciness and seasoning according to your taste preferences. Enjoy!

Sannakji

Ingredients:

- Live baby octopus (sannakji)
- Sesame oil
- Soy sauce
- Korean red chili flakes (gochugaru)
- Sesame seeds
- Thinly sliced green onions (optional)
- Thinly sliced garlic (optional)

Instructions:

1. Prepare the Octopus:
    - Ensure that you are working with fresh, live baby octopus. Rinse them thoroughly under cold water to remove any dirt or debris.
    - Using a sharp knife, quickly and carefully cut the tentacles away from the body of the octopus. Be cautious as the tentacles may still be moving.
2. Serve:
    - Arrange the freshly cut octopus tentacles on a plate.
    - Optionally, garnish with thinly sliced green onions and garlic.
3. Season:
    - Drizzle sesame oil over the octopus tentacles.
    - Serve with soy sauce on the side for dipping.
    - Optionally, sprinkle Korean red chili flakes (gochugaru) and sesame seeds over the octopus for added flavor and spice.
4. Eat:
    - To enjoy sannakji, use chopsticks to pick up a piece of octopus tentacle. Dip it into the soy sauce and sesame oil mixture.
    - Chew carefully as the octopus may still be moving due to nerve activity. Some people enjoy the sensation of the tentacles sticking to their mouth as they eat.
5. Enjoy Responsibly:
    - Please exercise caution when preparing and consuming live octopus. Ensure that you are purchasing fresh octopus from a reputable source and handle it safely to avoid injury.
    - It's also important to chew thoroughly to avoid choking hazards.

Sannakji is a unique and adventurous dish that is often enjoyed as a delicacy in Korea. It's not only about the flavor but also the experience of eating something alive and fresh. If you're open to trying new culinary experiences, sannakji could be an exciting dish to explore.

Budae Jjigae

Ingredients:

- 200g SPAM or ham, sliced
- 200g sausage or hot dogs, sliced
- 200g tofu, sliced
- 1 cup kimchi, chopped
- 1 onion, sliced
- 2 cloves garlic, minced
- 4 cups chicken or beef broth
- 2 cups water
- 2 tablespoons gochujang (Korean red chili paste)
- 1 tablespoon gochugaru (Korean red chili flakes)
- 2 tablespoons soy sauce
- 1 tablespoon sesame oil
- 1 tablespoon sugar
- 1 cup sliced mushrooms (such as shiitake or button mushrooms)
- 1 cup sliced cabbage or napa cabbage
- 1 cup sliced scallions
- 1 cup instant ramen noodles (optional)
- Salt and pepper to taste

Instructions:

1. Prepare the Ingredients:
    - Slice the SPAM or ham, sausage or hot dogs, tofu, onion, and mushrooms.
    - Chop the kimchi and slice the cabbage.
    - Mince the garlic and slice the scallions.
2. Make the Broth:
    - In a large pot, combine the chicken or beef broth, water, minced garlic, gochujang, gochugaru, soy sauce, sesame oil, and sugar. Bring to a boil over medium-high heat.
3. Add Ingredients to the Pot:
    - Add the sliced SPAM or ham, sausage or hot dogs, tofu, kimchi, onion, mushrooms, and cabbage to the pot. Stir well to combine.
4. Simmer:
    - Reduce the heat to medium-low and let the stew simmer for about 20-30 minutes, allowing the flavors to meld together and the ingredients to cook through.

5. Add Scallions and Noodles:
   - Add the sliced scallions to the stew during the last few minutes of cooking.
   - If using instant ramen noodles, add them to the stew during the last 3-4 minutes of cooking, stirring occasionally to ensure they cook evenly.
6. Adjust Seasoning:
   - Taste the budae jjigae and adjust the seasoning with salt and pepper if needed. The kimchi and gochujang may already add saltiness to the stew, so be mindful of the salt content.
7. Serve:
   - Ladle the hot budae jjigae into individual bowls and serve immediately.

Budae jjigae is a hearty and comforting stew that's perfect for sharing with family and friends. It's a versatile dish, so feel free to customize it with your favorite ingredients and adjust the spiciness according to your taste preferences. Enjoy!

Dakjuk

Ingredients:

- 1 cup short-grain white rice
- 4 cups water or chicken broth
- 1 chicken breast or thigh, boneless and skinless
- 1 tablespoon vegetable oil
- 2 cloves garlic, minced
- 1 teaspoon ginger, minced
- 4 cups water or chicken broth (additional, if needed)
- Salt and pepper to taste
- Thinly sliced green onions for garnish
- Toasted sesame seeds for garnish
- Sesame oil for drizzling (optional)

Instructions:

1. Prepare the Rice and Chicken:
    - Rinse the short-grain white rice under cold water until the water runs clear. Drain well.
    - In a pot, combine the rinsed rice with 4 cups of water or chicken broth. Bring to a boil over high heat, then reduce the heat to low and let it simmer, covered, for about 20-25 minutes, or until the rice is cooked and softened.
2. Cook the Chicken:
    - While the rice is cooking, cut the chicken breast or thigh into small bite-sized pieces.
    - In a separate skillet, heat the vegetable oil over medium heat. Add the minced garlic and ginger, and sauté for about 1 minute until fragrant.
    - Add the chicken pieces to the skillet and cook until they are no longer pink and have started to brown slightly.
3. Combine Rice and Chicken:
    - Once the rice is cooked, add the cooked chicken pieces along with any juices from the skillet into the pot of rice.
    - If the porridge is too thick, you can add additional water or chicken broth to reach your desired consistency.
4. Season:
    - Season the dakjuk with salt and pepper to taste. Adjust the seasoning according to your preference.
5. Simmer:

- Let the dakjuk simmer for another 5-10 minutes, stirring occasionally, to allow the flavors to meld together.
6. Serve:
    - Ladle the hot dakjuk into individual serving bowls.
    - Garnish with thinly sliced green onions and toasted sesame seeds.
    - Optionally, drizzle a little sesame oil over the top for extra flavor.

Dakjuk is best enjoyed hot and can be served as a comforting meal on its own or accompanied by side dishes such as kimchi or pickled vegetables. It's a simple and nourishing dish that's sure to warm you up on a chilly day. Enjoy!

Hobakjuk

Ingredients:

- 1 small pumpkin (about 2-3 pounds)
- 1/2 cup glutinous rice flour (also known as sweet rice flour)
- 4 cups water
- 1/4 cup sugar (adjust to taste)
- Pinch of salt
- Optional toppings: toasted pumpkin seeds, cinnamon powder, or chopped nuts

Instructions:

1. Prepare the Pumpkin:
    - Cut the pumpkin in half and remove the seeds and strings.
    - Peel the pumpkin and cut it into small cubes.
2. Cook the Pumpkin:
    - In a large pot, bring 4 cups of water to a boil.
    - Add the cubed pumpkin to the boiling water and cook until tender, about 15-20 minutes.
3. Puree the Pumpkin:
    - Once the pumpkin is soft, use a blender or immersion blender to puree it until smooth. Alternatively, you can mash the pumpkin with a potato masher.
4. Make the Porridge:
    - In a small bowl, mix the glutinous rice flour with a little water to form a smooth paste.
    - Gradually whisk the rice flour paste into the pureed pumpkin, stirring constantly to prevent lumps from forming.
5. Cook the Porridge:
    - Bring the pumpkin mixture to a gentle boil over medium heat, stirring frequently to prevent sticking.
    - Reduce the heat to low and let the porridge simmer for about 10-15 minutes, stirring occasionally, until it thickens to your desired consistency.
6. Sweeten and Season:
    - Add sugar and a pinch of salt to the porridge, adjusting the sweetness to your taste. Stir until the sugar is dissolved.
7. Serve:
    - Ladle the hot hobakjuk into individual serving bowls.

- Garnish with toasted pumpkin seeds, a sprinkle of cinnamon powder, or chopped nuts if desired.
- Serve the hobakjuk warm and enjoy as a comforting dessert or snack.

Hobakjuk is a delightful and nutritious dish that's perfect for warming up on a chilly day. The creamy texture and subtle sweetness of the pumpkin make it a comforting treat for any occasion. Enjoy!

Kongnamul Guk

Ingredients:

- 4 cups soybean sprouts (kongnamul)
- 6 cups water
- 4 garlic cloves, minced
- 2 green onions, thinly sliced
- 1 tablespoon sesame oil
- 1 tablespoon soy sauce
- Salt, to taste
- Optional: 4 dried anchovies (remove heads and guts)
- Optional: 100g beef (thinly sliced)

Instructions:

1. Rinse the soybean sprouts under cold water and remove any damaged or discolored sprouts. Trim off any roots or tough ends.
2. In a large pot, bring the water to a boil. If using dried anchovies, add them to the boiling water and let them simmer for about 5 minutes to create a flavorful broth. Then, remove and discard the anchovies.
3. Add the soybean sprouts to the pot of boiling water. Let them cook for about 5-7 minutes until they are tender but still slightly crunchy.
4. If using beef, add the thinly sliced beef to the pot and cook until it's no longer pink.
5. Reduce the heat to medium-low and add the minced garlic, sliced green onions, sesame oil, and soy sauce to the pot. Let the soup simmer for an additional 5 minutes to allow the flavors to meld together.
6. Taste the soup and adjust the seasoning with salt if needed.
7. Serve the Kongnamul Guk hot as a side dish or as part of a larger Korean meal. Enjoy!

Feel free to adjust the ingredients and seasonings according to your taste preferences.

Enjoy your homemade Kongnamul Guk!

Gamjatang

Ingredients:

- 2 lbs pork neck bones or pork spine bones, cut into pieces
- 1 onion, quartered
- 4 cloves garlic, minced
- 2 potatoes, peeled and cut into chunks
- 2 cups cabbage, chopped
- 1 cup Korean radish (mu), sliced
- 4 green onions, cut into 2-inch pieces
- 1/4 cup Korean soybean paste (doenjang)
- 3 tablespoons Korean hot pepper paste (gochujang)
- 1 tablespoon Korean chili flakes (gochugaru)
- 1 tablespoon soy sauce
- 1 tablespoon sesame oil
- Salt and pepper, to taste
- Water

Instructions:

1. In a large pot, add the pork bones and enough water to cover them completely. Bring to a boil over high heat, then reduce the heat to medium-low and simmer for about 20 minutes. This helps to remove any impurities from the bones.
2. Drain the bones and rinse them under cold water. Clean the pot and return the bones to it.
3. Add fresh water to the pot, enough to cover the bones again. Add the quartered onion and minced garlic. Bring to a boil, then reduce the heat to low and simmer, partially covered, for about 1 to 1.5 hours until the meat is tender and falling off the bones.
4. Skim off any foam or impurities that rise to the surface of the soup during cooking.
5. Once the pork is tender, add the chopped potatoes, cabbage, Korean radish, and green onions to the pot. Simmer for an additional 20-30 minutes until the vegetables are cooked through.
6. In a small bowl, mix together the Korean soybean paste (doenjang), Korean hot pepper paste (gochujang), Korean chili flakes (gochugaru), soy sauce, and sesame oil to make a seasoning paste.

7. Add the seasoning paste to the soup and stir well to combine. Taste and adjust the seasoning with salt and pepper if needed.
8. Continue to simmer the soup for another 10-15 minutes to allow the flavors to meld together.
9. Serve the Gamjatang hot in individual bowls. It's often accompanied by a bowl of rice and side dishes like kimchi. Enjoy!

Feel free to adjust the spiciness level according to your preference by adding more or less Korean chili flakes or hot pepper paste. You can also add other vegetables like zucchini or mushrooms if desired.

Dotorimuk

Ingredients:

- 1 cup acorn starch (dotori garu)
- 4 cups water
- 1 tablespoon soy sauce
- 1 tablespoon sesame oil
- 1 tablespoon sesame seeds, toasted
- 2 green onions, thinly sliced
- Optional: 1 tablespoon gochugaru (Korean chili flakes)
- Optional: 1 tablespoon vinegar
- Optional: 1 tablespoon sugar
- Salt, to taste

Instructions:

1. In a large mixing bowl, combine the acorn starch and water. Stir well to dissolve the starch completely. Let it sit for about 5 minutes to allow any impurities to settle at the bottom.
2. Carefully pour off the top liquid, leaving behind the settled starch at the bottom. Repeat this process 2-3 times until the water is clear and the settled starch is all that remains.
3. Transfer the clear starch to a pot and bring it to a gentle boil over medium heat, stirring constantly to prevent lumps from forming.
4. Once the mixture starts to thicken and become translucent, reduce the heat to low and continue to cook for another 5-10 minutes, stirring constantly, until it becomes a thick, gel-like consistency.
5. Remove the pot from the heat and pour the thickened mixture into a shallow dish or mold. Smooth out the surface with a spatula and let it cool to room temperature. Then, refrigerate for at least 2 hours or until completely set.
6. Once the acorn jelly has set, cut it into bite-sized cubes or slices.
7. In a separate bowl, mix together the soy sauce, sesame oil, toasted sesame seeds, and sliced green onions to make a seasoning sauce.
8. Arrange the dotorimuk slices on a serving plate and drizzle the seasoning sauce over the top. If desired, you can also sprinkle some gochugaru for extra spice or add a combination of vinegar and sugar for a tangy flavor.
9. Serve the Dotorimuk chilled as a side dish or as part of a Korean meal. Enjoy!

Feel free to adjust the seasoning sauce according to your taste preferences. You can also add other ingredients like sliced cucumbers, carrots, or hard-boiled eggs to create a more elaborate salad with Dotorimuk as the base.

Gyeranjjim

Ingredients:

- 4 large eggs
- 1 cup water or broth (chicken or vegetable)
- 1 tablespoon soy sauce
- 1 tablespoon sesame oil
- 1 green onion, thinly sliced (optional)
- Salt and pepper, to taste
- Toasted sesame seeds, for garnish (optional)

Instructions:

1. In a mixing bowl, crack the eggs and beat them until well combined.
2. Add the water or broth to the beaten eggs and mix thoroughly. The addition of broth adds extra flavor to the dish, but water works just fine as well.
3. Season the egg mixture with soy sauce, sesame oil, salt, and pepper. Adjust the seasoning according to your taste preferences. If using broth, adjust the salt accordingly as the broth may already be seasoned.
4. Strain the egg mixture through a fine mesh sieve or strainer into a heatproof bowl or dish. This helps to remove any foam or impurities and ensures a smoother texture for the Gyeranjjim.
5. If desired, add thinly sliced green onions to the egg mixture for extra flavor and color.
6. Prepare a steamer by bringing water to a boil in a pot or steamer basket.
7. Once the water is boiling, carefully place the bowl or dish with the strained egg mixture into the steamer. Cover with a lid and steam over medium heat for about 10-15 minutes, or until the eggs are set and slightly puffed up.
8. To check if the Gyeranjjim is cooked through, insert a toothpick or knife into the center. If it comes out clean, the dish is ready.
9. Once cooked, remove the Gyeranjjim from the steamer and garnish with toasted sesame seeds, if desired.
10. Serve the Gyeranjjim hot as a side dish or as part of a Korean meal. Enjoy its light and fluffy texture with the savory flavors of soy sauce and sesame oil!

Feel free to customize your Gyeranjjim by adding other ingredients like diced vegetables, cooked meat, or seafood for extra flavor and texture.

Miyeokguk

Ingredients:

- 1 cup dried miyeok (seaweed)
- 6 cups water
- 2 tablespoons sesame oil
- 2 cloves garlic, minced
- 1 tablespoon soy sauce
- Salt, to taste
- 2 cups cooked rice (optional)
- 2 green onions, thinly sliced (optional)
- Toasted sesame seeds, for garnish (optional)

Instructions:

1. Rinse the dried miyeok (seaweed) under cold water to remove any debris. Soak the miyeok in water for about 20-30 minutes, or until it becomes soft and pliable. Drain and cut the softened miyeok into bite-sized pieces.
2. In a large pot, bring 6 cups of water to a boil over medium-high heat. Add the soaked and cut miyeok to the pot and let it simmer for about 15-20 minutes, or until the seaweed is tender.
3. While the miyeok is simmering, heat sesame oil in a separate pan over medium heat. Add minced garlic and sauté until fragrant, about 1-2 minutes.
4. Add the sautéed garlic and sesame oil to the pot of simmering miyeok. Stir in soy sauce and salt to taste. Adjust the seasoning according to your preference.
5. If desired, add cooked rice to the soup to make it more substantial. Let the soup simmer for an additional 5-10 minutes to allow the flavors to meld together.
6. Once the soup is ready, ladle it into serving bowls. Garnish with thinly sliced green onions and toasted sesame seeds, if desired.
7. Serve the Miyeokguk hot as a main dish or as part of a Korean meal. It's often accompanied by a bowl of rice and side dishes like kimchi. Enjoy the nourishing and comforting flavors of this traditional Korean seaweed soup!

Feel free to customize your Miyeokguk by adding other ingredients such as tofu, beef, or vegetables like mushrooms or carrots for extra flavor and nutrition.

Ojingeo bokkeum

Ingredients:

- 1 lb fresh squid (cleaned and prepared)
- 2 tablespoons vegetable oil
- 1 onion, thinly sliced
- 1 bell pepper, thinly sliced
- 2-3 green onions, cut into 2-inch pieces
- 4 cloves garlic, minced
- 2 tablespoons gochujang (Korean chili paste)
- 1 tablespoon soy sauce
- 1 tablespoon sugar
- 1 tablespoon sesame oil
- Sesame seeds, for garnish
- Optional: 1 tablespoon gochugaru (Korean chili flakes) for extra spiciness

Instructions:

1. Prepare the squid by cleaning it thoroughly and cutting it into bite-sized pieces. If using frozen squid, make sure to thaw it completely before cooking.
2. Heat vegetable oil in a large skillet or wok over medium-high heat. Add the sliced onion and bell pepper to the skillet and stir-fry for 2-3 minutes until they start to soften.
3. Add the minced garlic to the skillet and stir-fry for another 1-2 minutes until fragrant.
4. Add the prepared squid to the skillet and stir-fry for 3-4 minutes until it turns opaque and starts to curl. Be careful not to overcook the squid, as it can become tough.
5. In a small bowl, mix together the gochujang, soy sauce, sugar, and sesame oil to make the sauce.
6. Pour the sauce over the squid and vegetables in the skillet. Stir well to coat everything evenly in the sauce.
7. If desired, add gochugaru for extra spiciness and stir to incorporate.
8. Continue to stir-fry for another 2-3 minutes until the sauce has thickened slightly and everything is well combined.
9. Remove the skillet from heat and transfer the Ojingeo bokkeum to a serving plate.

10. Garnish with sliced green onions and sesame seeds.
11. Serve the Ojingeo bokkeum hot as a main dish, accompanied by steamed rice and other side dishes. Enjoy the spicy and flavorful stir-fried squid!

Feel free to adjust the spiciness level of the dish by adding more or less gochujang and gochugaru according to your taste preferences. You can also add other vegetables like carrots, zucchini, or mushrooms for extra flavor and texture.

Kimchi fried rice

Ingredients:

- 2 cups cooked rice (preferably day-old rice)
- 1 cup kimchi, chopped
- 2 tablespoons kimchi juice (from the kimchi jar)
- 2 tablespoons vegetable oil
- 1 small onion, diced
- 2 cloves garlic, minced
- 1 tablespoon soy sauce
- 1 teaspoon sesame oil
- 1/2 cup cooked protein of your choice (such as diced chicken, pork, tofu, or shrimp)
- 2 green onions, thinly sliced
- Optional: 1 tablespoon gochujang (Korean chili paste) for extra spiciness
- Optional toppings: fried egg, toasted sesame seeds, sliced nori (seaweed), sliced cucumber

Instructions:

1. Heat vegetable oil in a large skillet or wok over medium heat. Add diced onion and minced garlic to the skillet and sauté for 2-3 minutes until softened and fragrant.
2. Add chopped kimchi to the skillet and stir-fry for another 2-3 minutes until heated through and slightly caramelized.
3. If using, add gochujang to the skillet and stir to incorporate.
4. Add cooked rice to the skillet, breaking up any clumps with a spatula. Stir-fry the rice with the kimchi mixture for 3-4 minutes until the rice is heated through and evenly coated with the kimchi.
5. Drizzle soy sauce, sesame oil, and kimchi juice over the rice mixture. Stir well to combine.
6. Add the cooked protein of your choice (chicken, pork, tofu, shrimp, etc.) to the skillet and stir-fry for another 2-3 minutes until heated through.
7. Taste the fried rice and adjust the seasoning if needed, adding more soy sauce or kimchi juice if desired.
8. Remove the skillet from heat and garnish the Kimchi fried rice with thinly sliced green onions.

9. Serve the Kimchi fried rice hot as a main dish, optionally topped with a fried egg, toasted sesame seeds, sliced nori, or sliced cucumber.
10. Enjoy the delicious and flavorful Kimchi fried rice as a satisfying meal!

Bulgogi bibimbap

Ingredients for Bulgogi:

- 1 lb thinly sliced beef (such as sirloin or ribeye)
- 1/4 cup soy sauce
- 2 tablespoons brown sugar
- 2 tablespoons sesame oil
- 2 cloves garlic, minced
- 1 tablespoon grated ginger
- 2 green onions, chopped
- 1 tablespoon toasted sesame seeds
- 1 tablespoon rice wine (mirin) or apple juice (optional)
- 1 tablespoon vegetable oil (for cooking)

Ingredients for Bibimbap:

- Cooked rice (1 cup per serving)
- Assorted vegetables (such as spinach, carrots, bean sprouts, mushrooms, zucchini, and lettuce)
- 4 eggs
- Kimchi (optional)
- Toasted sesame seeds (for garnish)
- Korean chili paste (gochujang) or sauce (optional)

Instructions:

1. Marinate the beef: In a bowl, combine soy sauce, brown sugar, sesame oil, minced garlic, grated ginger, chopped green onions, toasted sesame seeds, and rice wine or apple juice (if using). Add the thinly sliced beef to the marinade and mix until well coated. Let it marinate for at least 30 minutes, or preferably overnight in the refrigerator.
2. Cook the marinated beef: Heat vegetable oil in a large skillet or wok over medium-high heat. Add the marinated beef to the skillet and cook for 3-4 minutes until browned and cooked through. Remove from heat and set aside.
3. Prepare the vegetables: Wash and prepare the assorted vegetables. You can blanch or stir-fry them individually with a bit of oil and salt until tender-crisp.

4. Cook the eggs: In a separate non-stick pan, fry the eggs sunny-side up or over-easy.
5. Assemble the bibimbap: Divide the cooked rice among serving bowls. Arrange the cooked beef and assorted vegetables on top of the rice in separate sections. Add a spoonful of kimchi if desired. Place a fried egg on top of each bowl.
6. Serve the bibimbap: Garnish with toasted sesame seeds and serve hot. Optionally, serve with Korean chili paste (gochujang) or sauce on the side for extra flavor and spice. Before eating, mix everything together thoroughly to combine the flavors.
7. Enjoy your homemade Bulgogi bibimbap!

Kimchi pancakes

Ingredients:

- 1 cup kimchi, chopped
- 1 cup all-purpose flour
- 1/2 cup water
- 1 egg
- 2 tablespoons kimchi juice (from the kimchi jar)
- 2 green onions, thinly sliced
- 1 tablespoon soy sauce
- 1 tablespoon sesame oil
- 1 tablespoon vegetable oil (for frying)
- Optional: chopped vegetables like onions, carrots, or bell peppers
- Optional: thinly sliced pork or tofu for added protein
- Optional dipping sauce: soy sauce mixed with vinegar, sesame oil, and toasted sesame seeds

Instructions:

1. In a large mixing bowl, combine chopped kimchi, all-purpose flour, water, egg, kimchi juice, thinly sliced green onions, soy sauce, and sesame oil. Mix well until a smooth batter forms. If the batter is too thick, you can add a bit more water to reach the desired consistency.
2. If using any additional ingredients like chopped vegetables or protein, fold them into the batter.
3. Heat vegetable oil in a non-stick skillet or frying pan over medium heat.
4. Once the oil is hot, pour a ladleful of the kimchi batter into the skillet, spreading it out into a round pancake shape using the back of the ladle.
5. Cook the pancake for 3-4 minutes on each side, or until golden brown and crispy.
6. Repeat the process with the remaining batter, adding more oil to the skillet as needed.
7. Once all the pancakes are cooked, transfer them to a serving plate and cut them into wedges.
8. Serve the Kimchi pancakes hot with your favorite dipping sauce on the side.
9. Enjoy the crispy and flavorful Kimchi pancakes as a delicious appetizer, snack, or side dish!

Feel free to customize your Kimchi pancakes by adding other ingredients like seafood, shredded cheese, or additional spices according to your taste preferences. They're versatile and can be enjoyed on their own or as part of a larger Korean meal.

Gamja jeon

Ingredients:

- 2 large potatoes, peeled and grated
- 1 small onion, finely chopped
- 2 green onions, thinly sliced
- 2 tablespoons all-purpose flour or potato starch
- 1 egg, beaten
- 1/2 teaspoon salt
- 1/4 teaspoon black pepper
- Vegetable oil, for frying
- Optional: dipping sauce (soy sauce, vinegar, sesame oil, and sesame seeds)

Instructions:

1. Peel the potatoes and grate them using a box grater or a food processor. Place the grated potatoes in a clean kitchen towel or cheesecloth and squeeze out excess moisture.
2. In a large mixing bowl, combine the grated potatoes, chopped onion, sliced green onions, all-purpose flour or potato starch, beaten egg, salt, and black pepper. Mix well until everything is evenly combined.
3. Heat vegetable oil in a non-stick skillet or frying pan over medium heat.
4. Once the oil is hot, scoop a spoonful of the potato mixture and gently place it into the skillet, flattening it slightly with the back of the spoon to form a pancake shape.
5. Cook the pancakes for 3-4 minutes on each side, or until golden brown and crispy. Press down gently with a spatula to ensure even cooking.
6. Repeat the process with the remaining potato mixture, adding more oil to the skillet as needed.
7. Once all the pancakes are cooked, transfer them to a serving plate lined with paper towels to drain excess oil.
8. Serve the Gamja jeon hot with your favorite dipping sauce on the side.
9. Enjoy the crispy and flavorful Korean potato pancakes as a delicious appetizer, snack, or side dish!

Feel free to customize your Gamja jeon by adding other ingredients like shredded carrots, garlic, or chili peppers according to your taste preferences. They're versatile and can be enjoyed on their own or as part of a larger Korean meal.

Dubu kimchi

Ingredients:

- 1 block firm tofu, drained and cubed
- 1 cup kimchi, chopped
- 2 cloves garlic, minced
- 2 green onions, chopped
- 1 tablespoon soy sauce
- 1 tablespoon sesame oil
- 1 teaspoon sugar (optional)
- 1 teaspoon sesame seeds, for garnish
- Vegetable oil, for cooking

Instructions:

1. Drain the firm tofu and cut it into cubes. Pat the tofu cubes dry with paper towels to remove excess moisture.
2. Heat vegetable oil in a large skillet or frying pan over medium-high heat.
3. Once the oil is hot, add the tofu cubes to the skillet in a single layer. Fry the tofu cubes for 5-6 minutes on each side, or until golden brown and crispy. Remove the tofu cubes from the skillet and set them aside on a plate lined with paper towels to drain excess oil.
4. In the same skillet, add chopped kimchi and minced garlic. Stir-fry for 2-3 minutes until the kimchi is heated through and slightly caramelized.
5. Add the fried tofu cubes back to the skillet with the kimchi. Stir in soy sauce, sesame oil, and sugar (if using). Mix well to coat the tofu and kimchi evenly with the seasonings.
6. Cook for an additional 2-3 minutes, stirring occasionally, until the flavors are well combined.
7. Garnish the Dubu kimchi with chopped green onions and toasted sesame seeds.
8. Serve hot as a main dish or as a side dish with steamed rice.
9. Enjoy the flavorful and satisfying Dubu kimchi with its combination of crispy tofu and tangy kimchi!

Feel free to adjust the seasoning according to your taste preferences. You can also add other ingredients like sliced onions, mushrooms, or bell peppers for extra flavor and texture.

Nakji bokkeum

Ingredients:

- 1 lb fresh octopus (cleaned and prepared)
- 2 tablespoons vegetable oil
- 1 onion, thinly sliced
- 1 carrot, julienned
- 2-3 green onions, cut into 2-inch pieces
- 4 cloves garlic, minced
- 2 tablespoons gochujang (Korean chili paste)
- 1 tablespoon soy sauce
- 1 tablespoon sugar
- 1 tablespoon sesame oil
- Sesame seeds, for garnish

Instructions:

1. If using fresh octopus, clean it thoroughly and cut it into bite-sized pieces. If using frozen octopus, make sure to thaw it completely before cooking.
2. Heat vegetable oil in a large skillet or wok over medium-high heat. Add thinly sliced onion, julienned carrot, and cut green onions to the skillet. Stir-fry for 2-3 minutes until the vegetables start to soften.
3. Add minced garlic to the skillet and stir-fry for another 1-2 minutes until fragrant.
4. Add the prepared octopus to the skillet and stir-fry for 3-4 minutes until it turns opaque and starts to curl. Be careful not to overcook the octopus, as it can become tough.
5. In a small bowl, mix together gochujang, soy sauce, sugar, and sesame oil to make the sauce.
6. Pour the sauce over the octopus and vegetables in the skillet. Stir well to coat everything evenly in the sauce.
7. Continue to stir-fry for another 2-3 minutes until the sauce has thickened slightly and everything is well combined.
8. Remove the skillet from heat and transfer the Nakji bokkeum to a serving plate.
9. Garnish with sesame seeds.
10. Serve the Nakji bokkeum hot as a main dish, accompanied by steamed rice and other side dishes. Enjoy the spicy and flavorful stir-fried octopus!

Feel free to adjust the spiciness level of the dish by adding more or less gochujang according to your taste preferences. You can also add other vegetables like bell peppers, mushrooms, or zucchini for extra flavor and texture.

Gopchang jeongol

Ingredients:

- 1 lb gopchang (beef or pork small intestines), cleaned and cut into bite-sized pieces
- 4 cups beef or pork broth (you can use store-bought or homemade)
- 1 onion, sliced
- 1 carrot, sliced
- 1 potato, peeled and cubed
- 4-5 shiitake mushrooms, sliced
- 1/2 block firm tofu, cubed
- 4 cloves garlic, minced
- 2 green onions, cut into 2-inch pieces
- 1 tablespoon sesame oil
- 1 tablespoon soy sauce
- 1 tablespoon Korean chili paste (gochujang)
- 1 tablespoon Korean chili flakes (gochugaru)
- Salt and pepper, to taste
- Optional: sliced cabbage, enoki mushrooms, rice cakes (tteok)

Instructions:

1. In a large pot or Korean earthenware pot (dolsot), bring the beef or pork broth to a boil over medium-high heat.
2. Add the cleaned and cut gopchang pieces to the boiling broth. Let it cook for about 5 minutes to remove any impurities. Skim off any foam that rises to the surface.
3. Add the sliced onion, carrot, potato, shiitake mushrooms, tofu, minced garlic, and green onions to the pot.
4. Stir in sesame oil, soy sauce, Korean chili paste (gochujang), and Korean chili flakes (gochugaru) to the pot. Mix well to combine all the ingredients.
5. Cover the pot and let the stew simmer over medium heat for about 20-25 minutes, or until the vegetables are tender and the gopchang is cooked through.
6. Taste the stew and adjust the seasoning with salt and pepper if needed.
7. If using optional ingredients like sliced cabbage, enoki mushrooms, or rice cakes (tteok), add them to the pot during the last 5-10 minutes of cooking.
8. Once the stew is cooked and all the ingredients are tender, remove it from heat.

9. Serve the Gopchang jeongol hot in individual bowls. It's often accompanied by steamed rice and side dishes like kimchi.
10. Enjoy the hearty and flavorful Gopchang jeongol with its tender small intestines and assorted vegetables in a rich and spicy broth!

Haejangguk

Ingredients:

- 1 lb beef brisket or beef bones
- 8 cups water
- 2 tablespoons soy sauce
- 1 onion, quartered
- 4 cloves garlic, smashed
- 2 green onions, cut into 2-inch pieces
- 1 small piece of ginger, sliced
- 1 tablespoon Korean soybean paste (doenjang)
- 1 tablespoon Korean chili paste (gochujang)
- 1 cup napa cabbage, chopped
- 1 cup daikon radish, sliced
- 1 cup Korean radish greens or spinach, chopped
- 1 cup Korean glass noodles (dangmyeon), soaked in water until softened
- Salt and pepper, to taste
- Optional: sliced mushrooms, tofu, cooked rice cakes (tteok)

Instructions:

1. In a large pot, combine beef brisket or beef bones with water, soy sauce, quartered onion, smashed garlic cloves, green onions, and ginger slices. Bring to a boil over high heat.
2. Once boiling, reduce the heat to low and let the broth simmer for about 1 to 1.5 hours, skimming off any foam or impurities that rise to the surface.
3. Remove the beef brisket or bones from the broth and set aside to cool. Strain the broth through a fine mesh sieve or cheesecloth to remove any solids, then return it to the pot.
4. While the broth is simmering, shred the cooked beef brisket or remove the meat from the bones and set aside.
5. Stir in Korean soybean paste (doenjang) and Korean chili paste (gochujang) into the broth until fully dissolved, adding more to taste if desired.
6. Add chopped napa cabbage, sliced daikon radish, and chopped Korean radish greens or spinach to the pot. Let them simmer for about 10-15 minutes until tender.

7. Drain the soaked Korean glass noodles (dangmyeon) and add them to the pot, stirring gently to incorporate.
8. Return the shredded beef or meat pieces to the pot. Add any optional ingredients like sliced mushrooms, tofu, or cooked rice cakes (tteok) if desired.
9. Season the soup with salt and pepper to taste. Allow it to simmer for an additional 5-10 minutes to let the flavors meld together.
10. Serve the Haejangguk hot in individual bowls. Enjoy the comforting and revitalizing effects of this traditional Korean hangover soup!

Japchae bap

Ingredients:

- 1 lb Korean glass noodles (dangmyeon)
- 1 lb beef (ribeye, sirloin, or tenderloin), thinly sliced
- 1 onion, thinly sliced
- 2 carrots, julienned
- 1 red bell pepper, thinly sliced
- 1 yellow bell pepper, thinly sliced
- 4-5 shiitake mushrooms, sliced
- 4 cloves garlic, minced
- 4 tablespoons soy sauce
- 2 tablespoons sugar
- 2 tablespoons sesame oil
- 2 tablespoons vegetable oil
- Salt and pepper, to taste
- Cooked rice, for serving
- Toasted sesame seeds, for garnish
- Thinly sliced green onions, for garnish

Instructions:

1. Cook the Korean glass noodles (dangmyeon) according to the package instructions until they are fully cooked but still slightly chewy. Drain and rinse under cold water to stop the cooking process. Set aside.
2. In a bowl, combine thinly sliced beef with minced garlic, soy sauce, sugar, and sesame oil. Mix well to ensure the beef is evenly coated with the marinade. Let it marinate for about 20-30 minutes.
3. Heat vegetable oil in a large skillet or wok over medium-high heat. Add the marinated beef to the skillet and stir-fry for 2-3 minutes until it is cooked through. Remove the beef from the skillet and set aside.
4. In the same skillet, add a bit more vegetable oil if needed. Stir-fry the sliced onion, julienned carrots, sliced bell peppers, and shiitake mushrooms for 3-4 minutes until they are tender-crisp.
5. Add the cooked Korean glass noodles (dangmyeon) to the skillet with the vegetables. Stir-fry everything together for another 2-3 minutes until the noodles are heated through and well combined with the vegetables.

6. Return the cooked beef to the skillet with the noodles and vegetables. Stir-fry everything together for another minute to heat through.
7. Taste and adjust the seasoning with salt, pepper, or additional soy sauce if needed.
8. Serve the Japchae bap hot over cooked rice in individual bowls. Garnish with toasted sesame seeds and thinly sliced green onions.
9. Enjoy your homemade Japchae bap, a delicious fusion of stir-fried glass noodles and rice!

Seolleongtang

Ingredients:

- 2-3 lbs beef bones (such as ox bones or beef leg bones)
- 1 lb beef brisket or beef shank, thinly sliced
- 12 cups water
- 1 onion, halved
- 6 cloves garlic
- 1 piece ginger (about 1-inch), sliced
- Salt, to taste
- Thinly sliced green onions, for garnish
- Cooked rice, for serving
- Kimchi, for serving (optional)

Instructions:

1. Rinse the beef bones under cold water to remove any blood or impurities. Place the bones in a large pot and cover with cold water. Let them soak for 1-2 hours to remove excess blood.
2. Drain the bones and rinse them again under cold water. Transfer the bones to a clean pot.
3. Add 12 cups of water to the pot with the beef bones. Bring to a boil over high heat.
4. Once boiling, reduce the heat to low and let the broth simmer gently. Skim off any foam or impurities that rise to the surface.
5. Add the thinly sliced beef brisket or beef shank to the pot. Continue to simmer the broth for 3-4 hours, stirring occasionally, until the meat is tender and falls apart easily.
6. Add the halved onion, garlic cloves, and sliced ginger to the pot. Let the broth simmer for another 1-2 hours to infuse the flavors.
7. Once the broth is rich and flavorful, remove the beef bones and any large pieces of onion, garlic, or ginger from the pot. Discard them.
8. Season the broth with salt to taste. Adjust the seasoning according to your preference.
9. Ladle the Seolleongtang into individual serving bowls. Add a few slices of cooked beef brisket or beef shank to each bowl.
10. Garnish with thinly sliced green onions.
11. Serve the Seolleongtang hot with cooked rice and kimchi on the side, if desired.

12. Enjoy the comforting and nourishing Seolleongtang as a hearty meal!

Gyeran-mari

Ingredients:

- 4 large eggs
- 2 tablespoons water or milk
- Salt, to taste
- Black pepper, to taste
- 1/4 cup finely chopped vegetables (such as carrots, bell peppers, onions, spinach, or mushrooms)
- 1/4 cup finely chopped ham, cooked bacon, or cooked sausage (optional)
- 1 tablespoon vegetable oil

Instructions:

1. In a mixing bowl, crack the eggs and beat them lightly with a fork or whisk.
2. Add water or milk to the beaten eggs and mix well. The addition of water or milk helps to create a fluffy texture for the omelette.
3. Season the egg mixture with salt and black pepper to taste.
4. Add finely chopped vegetables and any optional fillings (such as ham, bacon, or sausage) to the egg mixture. Mix well to evenly distribute the ingredients.
5. Heat vegetable oil in a non-stick skillet or frying pan over medium heat.
6. Once the oil is hot, pour the egg mixture into the skillet, tilting the pan to spread the mixture evenly across the surface.
7. Cook the egg mixture for 2-3 minutes, lifting the edges with a spatula to allow the uncooked eggs to flow underneath.
8. Once the bottom of the omelette is set and lightly golden brown, carefully roll it up using a spatula or chopsticks.
9. Push the rolled omelette to one side of the skillet and add a bit more oil to the empty side if needed.
10. Pour the remaining egg mixture into the empty side of the skillet, tilting the pan to spread it evenly.
11. Cook the second layer of the omelette for another 2-3 minutes, lifting the edges with a spatula to allow the uncooked eggs to flow underneath.
12. Once the second layer is set and lightly golden brown, carefully roll it up again to form a thicker rolled omelette.
13. Remove the Gyeran-mari from the skillet and transfer it to a cutting board. Let it cool for a minute or two before slicing it into bite-sized pieces.

14. Serve the Gyeran-mari hot or at room temperature as a side dish or snack. Enjoy its fluffy texture and savory flavor!

Feel free to customize your Gyeran-mari by adding other ingredients like cheese, shrimp, or tofu for extra flavor and texture. You can also adjust the seasoning according to your taste preferences.

Godeungeo gui

Ingredients:

- 2 whole mackerel fish, cleaned and gutted
- 4 tablespoons soy sauce
- 2 tablespoons mirin (rice wine) or rice vinegar
- 2 tablespoons honey or brown sugar
- 2 cloves garlic, minced
- 1 tablespoon sesame oil
- 1 tablespoon sesame seeds
- Vegetable oil, for brushing the grill
- Optional: thinly sliced green onions or chopped cilantro for garnish

Instructions:

1. In a mixing bowl, combine soy sauce, mirin (or rice vinegar), honey (or brown sugar), minced garlic, sesame oil, and sesame seeds. Mix well to make the marinade.
2. Score the skin of the mackerel fish with a sharp knife on both sides. This will help the marinade penetrate the fish and prevent it from curling while grilling.
3. Place the cleaned mackerel fish in a shallow dish or a large resealable plastic bag. Pour the marinade over the fish, making sure it's evenly coated. Marinate the fish in the refrigerator for at least 30 minutes, or preferably 1-2 hours, to allow the flavors to develop.
4. Preheat your grill to medium-high heat. Brush the grill grates with vegetable oil to prevent the fish from sticking.
5. Once the grill is hot, carefully place the marinated mackerel fish on the grill grates, skin side down. Grill the fish for about 5-7 minutes on each side, or until the flesh is opaque and easily flakes with a fork. Be careful not to overcook the fish, as mackerel can become dry if cooked for too long.
6. While grilling, baste the fish with any remaining marinade to keep it moist and flavorful.
7. Once the fish is cooked through and has nice grill marks, remove it from the grill and transfer it to a serving platter.
8. Garnish the Godeungeo gui with thinly sliced green onions or chopped cilantro, if desired.
9. Serve the grilled mackerel hot with steamed rice and your favorite side dishes. Enjoy the savory and delicious flavor of Godeungeo gui straight from the grill!

Dakkochi

Ingredients:

- 1 lb boneless, skinless chicken thighs or breasts, cut into bite-sized pieces
- Bamboo skewers, soaked in water for 30 minutes to prevent burning
- For the marinade:
    - 1/4 cup soy sauce
    - 2 tablespoons brown sugar or honey
    - 1 tablespoon sesame oil
    - 1 tablespoon rice vinegar or apple cider vinegar
    - 2 cloves garlic, minced
    - 1 teaspoon grated ginger
    - 1 tablespoon gochujang (Korean chili paste) or Korean chili flakes (gochugaru) for spiciness (optional)
- For garnish:
    - Toasted sesame seeds
    - Thinly sliced green onions
    - Korean chili flakes (gochugaru) for extra spice (optional)

Instructions:

1. In a mixing bowl, combine soy sauce, brown sugar or honey, sesame oil, rice vinegar, minced garlic, grated ginger, and gochujang or Korean chili flakes (if using). Mix well to make the marinade.
2. Add the bite-sized chicken pieces to the marinade and toss to coat evenly. Cover the bowl with plastic wrap and refrigerate for at least 30 minutes, or preferably 1-2 hours, to allow the flavors to develop.
3. While the chicken is marinating, prepare your grill or preheat a grill pan or skillet over medium-high heat.
4. Thread the marinated chicken pieces onto the soaked bamboo skewers, leaving a little space between each piece.
5. Once the grill or skillet is hot, place the chicken skewers on the grill grates or in the skillet. Cook for about 3-4 minutes on each side, or until the chicken is cooked through and has nice grill marks.
6. While grilling, baste the chicken skewers with any remaining marinade to keep them moist and flavorful.
7. Once the chicken is cooked through, remove the skewers from the grill or skillet and transfer them to a serving platter.

8. Garnish the Dakkochi with toasted sesame seeds, thinly sliced green onions, and Korean chili flakes (gochugaru) for extra spice, if desired.
9. Serve the grilled chicken skewers hot as a delicious appetizer or main dish. Enjoy the savory and slightly sweet flavor of Dakkochi straight from the grill!

Hobak namul

Ingredients:

- 2 small zucchini (hobak), thinly sliced
- 2 cloves garlic, minced
- 1 tablespoon soy sauce
- 1 tablespoon sesame oil
- 1 teaspoon sesame seeds
- Salt, to taste
- Vegetable oil, for sautéing (if preferred)

Instructions:

1. Wash the zucchini thoroughly and cut off the ends. Slice the zucchini into thin, round pieces.
2. Fill a pot with water and bring it to a boil over high heat. Once boiling, add a pinch of salt to the water.
3. Blanch the sliced zucchini in the boiling water for about 1-2 minutes, or until they are just tender but still slightly crisp. Be careful not to overcook them. Alternatively, you can steam the zucchini slices for a few minutes until tender.
4. Drain the blanched or steamed zucchini slices and rinse them under cold water to stop the cooking process. Drain well and set aside.
5. In a small bowl, combine minced garlic, soy sauce, sesame oil, and sesame seeds to make the seasoning sauce.
6. Heat a small amount of vegetable oil in a skillet or frying pan over medium heat. If you prefer, you can skip this step and use the zucchini without sautéing.
7. Add the blanched or steamed zucchini slices to the skillet and sauté for 1-2 minutes, just until they are heated through.
8. Pour the seasoning sauce over the zucchini slices in the skillet. Toss gently to coat the zucchini evenly with the sauce.
9. Cook for another 1-2 minutes, stirring occasionally, until the zucchini is well coated with the seasoning sauce and heated through.
10. Taste the hobak namul and adjust the seasoning with salt if needed.
11. Once ready, transfer the hobak namul to a serving dish.
12. Serve the hobak namul warm or at room temperature as a side dish (banchan) with steamed rice and other Korean dishes. Enjoy the delicious flavor and tender texture of hobak namul!

Oi muchim

Ingredients:

- 2 medium-sized cucumbers
- 2 cloves garlic, minced
- 2 green onions, thinly sliced
- 1 tablespoon soy sauce
- 1 tablespoon rice vinegar or apple cider vinegar
- 1 tablespoon sesame oil
- 1 teaspoon sugar
- 1 teaspoon sesame seeds
- Pinch of salt, to taste
- Optional: thinly sliced red chili peppers or Korean chili flakes (gochugaru) for extra spice

Instructions:

1. Wash the cucumbers thoroughly and slice them thinly into rounds or julienne them into thin strips. Place the sliced cucumbers in a mixing bowl.
2. Sprinkle a pinch of salt over the sliced cucumbers and toss gently to coat. Let them sit for about 10-15 minutes to draw out excess moisture.
3. After 10-15 minutes, drain the excess liquid from the cucumbers and pat them dry with a clean kitchen towel or paper towels.
4. In a separate bowl, combine minced garlic, thinly sliced green onions, soy sauce, rice vinegar or apple cider vinegar, sesame oil, sugar, and sesame seeds. Mix well to make the seasoning sauce.
5. Pour the seasoning sauce over the sliced cucumbers in the mixing bowl. Toss gently to coat the cucumbers evenly with the sauce.
6. If desired, add thinly sliced red chili peppers or Korean chili flakes (gochugaru) for extra spice. Toss to combine.
7. Let the Oi muchim marinate for at least 10-15 minutes to allow the flavors to meld together.
8. Once ready, transfer the Oi muchim to a serving dish and garnish with additional sesame seeds or sliced green onions, if desired.
9. Serve the Oi muchim cold or at room temperature as a refreshing side dish (banchan) with steamed rice and other Korean dishes. Enjoy the crisp and tangy flavor of Oi muchim!

Oi-naengguk

Ingredients:

- 2 large cucumbers
- 4 cups water
- 2 tablespoons soy sauce
- 1 tablespoon rice vinegar or apple cider vinegar
- 1 tablespoon sugar
- 2 cloves garlic, minced
- 1 teaspoon sesame oil
- 1 teaspoon sesame seeds
- Salt, to taste
- Ice cubes, for serving
- Optional: thinly sliced green onions or chili peppers for garnish

Instructions:

1. Wash the cucumbers thoroughly and thinly slice them. You can use a knife or a mandoline slicer for even slices.
2. In a large mixing bowl, combine water, soy sauce, rice vinegar or apple cider vinegar, sugar, minced garlic, sesame oil, and sesame seeds. Mix well until the sugar is dissolved.
3. Add the sliced cucumbers to the bowl with the seasoned water mixture. Stir to combine.
4. Taste the soup and adjust the seasoning with salt if needed. Remember that the soup will be served cold, so it's okay for it to be slightly more seasoned than you would prefer.
5. Cover the bowl with plastic wrap or a lid and refrigerate for at least 1-2 hours to allow the flavors to meld together and the soup to chill.
6. Once the Oi-naengguk is well chilled and ready to serve, divide it into individual serving bowls.
7. Add a few ice cubes to each bowl to keep the soup cold and refreshing.
8. Garnish the Oi-naengguk with thinly sliced green onions or chili peppers, if desired.
9. Serve the Oi-naengguk cold as a refreshing side dish (banchan) alongside other Korean dishes. Enjoy its crisp and tangy flavor on a hot summer day!

Baek kimchi

Ingredients:

- 1 napa cabbage (about 2 pounds)
- 1 cup coarse sea salt
- 5 cups water
- 1 tablespoon sugar
- 1 daikon radish, julienned
- 2 carrots, julienned
- 4 green onions, sliced
- 4 cloves garlic, minced
- 1-inch piece of ginger, grated
- 1 tablespoon fish sauce (optional)
- 1 tablespoon salted shrimp (saeujeot) or anchovy sauce (optional)
- 2 tablespoons sesame seeds
- 1 tablespoon sesame oil

Instructions:

1. Cut the napa cabbage lengthwise into quarters. Remove the core from each quarter and chop the cabbage into bite-sized pieces.
2. In a large bowl, dissolve the coarse sea salt in water to create a brine. Submerge the chopped cabbage in the brine, making sure it's fully covered. Let it soak for 4-6 hours, turning occasionally.
3. Rinse the salted cabbage under cold water to remove excess salt. Drain well and set aside.
4. In a separate bowl, combine the sugar, minced garlic, grated ginger, fish sauce (if using), salted shrimp or anchovy sauce (if using), sesame seeds, and sesame oil. Mix well to create the seasoning paste.
5. Add the julienned daikon radish, carrots, and sliced green onions to the seasoning paste. Toss to coat the vegetables evenly.
6. Spread the seasoned vegetables between the cabbage leaves, layer by layer, making sure to distribute them evenly.
7. Tightly pack the seasoned cabbage and vegetables into a clean glass jar or airtight container. Press down firmly to remove any air pockets.
8. Cover the jar or container and let it ferment at room temperature for 1-2 days.

9. Once the baek kimchi has reached your desired level of fermentation, transfer it to the refrigerator to slow down the fermentation process and keep it fresh.
10. Serve baek kimchi chilled as a side dish (banchan) alongside rice and other Korean dishes. Enjoy its mild and refreshing flavor!

Jangjorim

Ingredients:

- 1 lb beef (brisket, flank steak, or shank), thinly sliced
- 4 cups water
- 1 cup soy sauce
- 1/2 cup mirin (rice wine) or cooking wine
- 1/4 cup sugar
- 4 cloves garlic, smashed
- 2 slices ginger
- 2 dried red chili peppers (optional, for extra spice)
- 2 green onions, cut into 2-inch pieces
- Hard-boiled eggs (optional)

Instructions:

1. In a large pot, combine water, soy sauce, mirin, sugar, smashed garlic cloves, ginger slices, and dried red chili peppers (if using). Bring the mixture to a boil over high heat.
2. Once boiling, reduce the heat to low and add the thinly sliced beef to the pot. Let it simmer gently for about 1.5 to 2 hours, uncovered, stirring occasionally.
3. After the beef has simmered and becomes tender, add the green onions to the pot and continue to simmer for another 10-15 minutes to infuse the flavors.
4. If desired, add hard-boiled eggs to the pot during the last 10-15 minutes of cooking to absorb the flavors of the broth.
5. Once the beef is tender and the broth has reduced and thickened slightly, remove the pot from heat.
6. Let the Jangjorim cool to room temperature before transferring it to a container with a lid.
7. Store the Jangjorim in the refrigerator for at least a few hours or overnight to allow the flavors to deepen.
8. Serve the Jangjorim chilled or at room temperature as a side dish (banchan) alongside steamed rice and other Korean dishes. Enjoy the savory and tender beef with its rich and flavorful broth!

Kimchi jigae

Ingredients:

- 2 cups well-fermented kimchi, chopped
- 200g pork belly or pork shoulder, thinly sliced
- 1 onion, thinly sliced
- 2 cloves garlic, minced
- 1 tablespoon gochujang (Korean chili paste)
- 1 tablespoon gochugaru (Korean chili flakes)
- 1 tablespoon soy sauce
- 1 tablespoon sesame oil
- 1 teaspoon sugar (optional)
- 2 cups vegetable or beef broth
- 1 block firm tofu, cut into cubes
- 2 green onions, chopped
- Sesame seeds, for garnish
- Cooked rice, for serving

Instructions:

1. Heat a large pot or deep skillet over medium heat. Add the thinly sliced pork and cook until it's browned and slightly crispy.
2. Add the minced garlic and sliced onion to the pot. Cook until the onion is translucent and fragrant.
3. Stir in the chopped kimchi, gochujang, and gochugaru. Cook for a few minutes until the kimchi is heated through and starts to soften.
4. Pour in the vegetable or beef broth. Bring the mixture to a boil, then reduce the heat to low and let it simmer for about 10-15 minutes to allow the flavors to meld together.
5. Taste the stew and adjust the seasoning with soy sauce and sugar, if needed, to balance the flavors.
6. Gently add the cubed tofu to the pot. Let it simmer for another 5-10 minutes until the tofu is heated through.
7. Stir in the chopped green onions and sesame oil. Remove the pot from heat.
8. Serve the Kimchi jigae hot in individual bowls, garnished with sesame seeds.
9. Enjoy your homemade Kimchi jigae with a bowl of steamed rice on the side. It's a comforting and satisfying meal, perfect for any day of the week!

Kimchi bokkeumbap

Ingredients:

- 3 cups cooked rice, preferably day-old
- 1 cup well-fermented kimchi, chopped
- 150g pork belly or bacon, diced (optional)
- 2 cloves garlic, minced
- 2 green onions, chopped
- 1 tablespoon vegetable oil
- 1 tablespoon sesame oil
- 1 tablespoon soy sauce
- 1 teaspoon sugar (optional)
- Sesame seeds, for garnish
- Fried eggs, for serving (optional)

Instructions:

1. Heat a large skillet or wok over medium heat. Add the vegetable oil and diced pork belly or bacon (if using). Cook until the meat is browned and crispy.
2. Add the minced garlic to the skillet and sauté for a minute until fragrant.
3. Stir in the chopped kimchi and cook for another 3-4 minutes until it's heated through and slightly caramelized.
4. Add the cooked rice to the skillet, breaking up any clumps with a spatula. Stir-fry everything together for 5-6 minutes until the rice is well coated with the kimchi mixture and starts to get slightly crispy.
5. Drizzle sesame oil and soy sauce over the rice. If desired, sprinkle sugar over the rice to balance the flavors. Mix well to combine.
6. Add chopped green onions to the skillet and stir-fry for another minute until everything is evenly mixed.
7. Taste the Kimchi bokkeumbap and adjust the seasoning with soy sauce or sugar if needed.
8. Remove the skillet from heat and transfer the Kimchi bokkeumbap to serving plates.
9. Garnish with sesame seeds and serve hot with fried eggs on top, if desired.
10. Enjoy your homemade Kimchi bokkeumbap as a delicious and satisfying meal!

www.ingramcontent.com/pod-product-compliance
Lightning Source LLC
LaVergne TN
LVHW061944070526
838199LV00060B/3958